It's All About
LOVE

A mother and her gay son's loving journey through the ravages of AIDS to the riches of heaven

* * *

by Elaine McKee Dancer

Copyright © 2013 Elaine McKee Dancer
All rights reserved.
ISBN: 1478280891
ISBN 13: 9781478280897
All scriptures are from the New International Version, copyright 1973,
International Bible Society unless otherwise noted.

IT'S ALL ABOUT LOVE

A mother and her gay son's loving journey
through the ravages of AIDS to the riches of heaven.

By

Elaine McKee Dancer

Dedication

To my beloved son Duane who lived life with such love and courage
And died with such grace and dignity.

To my late husband Dr. T. Dudley Dancer
who showed my son a father's love the last two years of his life.

Contents

Forward ix

Preface xiii

Acknowledgements xv

Chapter 1 – The Early Years 1

Chapter 2 – Duane's Coming-Out Party 15

Chapter 3 – Decisions–Right or Wrong 29

Chapter 4 – AIDS Strikes 49

Chapter 5 – Life Goes On 77

Chapter 6 – Mother–the Only One I Can Trust 95

Chapter 7 – Surprised by Love 103

Chapter 8 – Other Family Issues 119

Chapter 9 – My Reality for Now 129

Chapter 10 – Music to My Ears 139

Chapter 11 – On with His Spiritual Journey 153

Chapter 12 – The Final Days 159

Chapter 13 – Our Last Day–then Heaven 173

Appendix–Assurance of Heaven 185

FORWARD

Notes to Elaine

I am positive that your book will help to heal many wounds in people that cannot forgive or accept others; I have no doubt that you have a superior mission to accomplish, always guided by Jesus.

Love you so very much,

Juan (Duane's partner at the end of his life)

* * *

It's All About Love - An appropriate title as Elaine is all about love. I learned many lessons about love by watching Elaine and her son Duane. Elaine used love to fearlessly confront the conflict between her religious beliefs, her relationship with God and her relationship with her son, who was gay. Never giving up on either God or Duane, loving both she continued to stay in her love for both to work through painful times including Duane's death from HIV.

One teaching I received was Duane saying he could always trust his mother because she never wavered from who she was, despite the conflict, difference and risk presenting in their relationship. He could trust her and thus the relationship because she knew who she was.

Shahn McGuire
Licensed Marriage and Family Therapist

* * *

Hello Mother Dear!

It warms my heart and I cry tears of such happiness that I have you in my life. I consider myself extremely blessed to have been given the opportunity to know you. To feel the love you share and hold true to what you believe. To know that you were given the opportunity to spend time with your son, my friend in that last year of his life here on Earth is important to me. I know he knew he was loved unconditionally and without question. In that last year he was able to review and finish his "checklist" of things he needed to do in order to say goodbye. To feel your warm and tender hands on his tired little back as no other mother could do. To hold and be held lovingly before he closed his eyes and drifted peacefully asleep for the last time. I am so very grateful. Elaine Dancer you are an incredible mother, woman and friend and I do love you so.

Your faith and love of God has carried you and kept you whole when others would have surely crumbled. You are truly an amazing human being and I do love you so for being you and always treating me with such love, kindness and respect!

I will love you always!

Larry Dean Paszli (Duane's friend of many years)

* * *

With compassion and remarkable honesty, Elaine Dancer tells the story of her relationship with her precious son Duane as he passed from this life into eternity. This book is emotionally charged and speaks to how God blessed this mother/son relationship through unbelievable struggles.

    Carmyn Neely
    Lay Leader, Public Speaker, Life-long Educator

PREFACE

Thank you for reading our story; the story of my unconditional love for my son, even though I could not affirm his lifestyle. Just as no one is beyond God's love and grace, my love reached beyond Duane to his friends. Although we sometimes struggled, we enjoyed a fun, exciting life together.

Your faith may be different than mine. You may express it differently than I do. I pray that your faith gives you as much comfort as mine gives me.

This story has a beautiful ending of love and redemption. It is my desire that our story will encourage all families to love each other more and experience God's unconditional love and grace.

You may contact me at elaine@elainedancer.com

Acknowledgements

I appreciate the many people who knew Duane and me for the 35 years of his life, who offered their love and support, especially during the time of Duane's illness.

I would like to especially thank the following people, who encouraged and assisted in the writing of this book:

- My many faithful friends at Lover's Lane United Methodist Church and especially my pastor, Dr. Stanley Copeland, who encouraged me to tell my story.

- Linda Bedour, my neighbor, who continued to believe and challenge me.

- Jim Webb, my long-time friend, who always had faith in me and what I strived to accomplish.

- Linda Horseman for doing the difficult first editing.

- Marilyn Darnell Hood for assisting me with the final editing and formatting. She gave me the final push.

- The many people who through random meetings continued to ask me to write our story.

I feel the deepest gratitude for each of these individuals. I could not have written our story without their encouragement.

CHAPTER 1
The Early Years

* * *

It was an ordinary day, or so I thought, that the energetic young man with a blonde crew cut knocked at my door. Times were different then. You may remember Ozzie and Harriett from TV. You might say, that I was a Harriett "wanna be." I didn't work outside our home. I had given up my job and we were hoping to have a baby. Like Harriett, I got up each day, put on my makeup, dressed in something cute, put on my apron and often even heels. Yes, I was a 1962 Texas homemaker!

The young man at my door was a minister who was starting a new church in our neighborhood. This was my introduction not only to St. Paul's Methodist Church (later United Methodist), but to the minister, Dudley Dancer.

From the innocent moment when I answered the door and asked Dudley to come in, to this very day, there was no way I could know the impact he would have on my life.

Over the years, Dudley always said he remembered the red checked dress I was wearing that day as he sat at our table and visited over a cup of coffee.

My husband and I had just bought our first home. Jim had a good job at Collins Radio and was going to night school in Arlington.

I will never forget that home. It had three bedrooms, two baths, a small living room, a large dining room/den combination, a small kitchen, and a two-car garage. At $13,800, we had our mansion.

We had the house, a station wagon, the job, and were looking forward to having a child. What more could we have wanted? When you are young and in love and full of hopes and dreams, life can seem carefree and happy.

I loved my visit with Dudley that day, because I wanted to get back into a church. I had been raised in the Methodist Church. After Jim's stint in the Navy, during our first year in Texas, we didn't go to church much. I really missed it and Jim was glad to try the church that Dudley and his wife Sally were starting.

We all had a great time at the church. We cleaned the floors as well as the bathrooms. We taught Sunday school classes, and I was involved in the Women's Society of Christian Service, which evolved into the United Methodist Women.

We had lots of fun. The men had a baseball team, which Jim enjoyed a lot. Sally and Dudley would have us over to their house occasionally. You have probably heard of the coffee klatch era, where those of us who stayed at home instead of working outside our homes got together and laughed and told stories (some of which were probably just our imagination). Perhaps you wondered if they really happened. They did!

It was while having coffee with some neighbors in the fall of 1962 that I went to sleep sitting on the couch. This had happened several times. One of the girls said, "You must be pg." We did not say the word "pregnant" back in those days. My, how times have changed!

I can remember the day I went to the doctor. I had waited so long for this day. Over the years there were so many times I thought I might be expecting only to be disappointed. I told Dr. Campbell he better not tell me it was a false alarm. He assured me that, "Yes, I was going to have a baby!" I can still see myself walking down the sidewalk to my car, smiling from ear to ear. It was as though no one else had ever gotten this news before. I was elated! I thought Jim was too, but looking back, I am not sure.

My joy soon turned to concern. Starting with my third month, I tried to miscarry every month when I would have had a menstrual period. This required bed rest for about 10 days each month.

Jim was working during the daytime and driving to Arlington from Garland to attend college at night. Our families were all in Oklahoma, so there were a lot of lonely hours. My friend Marilyn, who lived across the street, was really good to me, but she was also expecting and had one little boy already, so she was limited to what she could do for me. Sometimes I would read, but much of the time I just lay there and prayed for my baby.

After I was allowed to get up, I could dust if I didn't bend over. The doctor wouldn't let me vacuum or pick up anything off the floor. Of course, lifting was out of the question. I am very thankful that Dr. Campbell was so strict with me. Otherwise, I might never have had my precious baby boy. Jim was very patient, never complaining about what I couldn't do.

Our pastor, Dudley, matured over the years, but even as a young man he was very compassionate. He came to Baylor Hospital when I was in labor since we had no family support. Jim went for coffee during his visit and Dudley sat with me.

I have to tell you, I did not want my pastor-friend in there with me. I was young, not quite 26, and I was very modest. Dudley was sitting up near my head. All at once, I had a really hard contraction and I reached out my hand and said, "Oh,

Dudley, hold my hand!" At that moment, I did not want to be alone.

Who could have ever guessed that Dudley would be my husband when that same precious baby would die at the age of 35? In 1963 when Duane was born we were all young and thought we would all grow old together, Dudley and Sally and Jim and me. Sometimes God has different plans.

For those of you who have had babies, I wonder what you remember about the birth of your children. One of the other things which is so vivid in my mind is the face of a nurse with bright red hair and brilliant green eye shadow. She asked how long I had been there. When Jim told her, she said, "Let's get this over."

The next thing I knew, they were hauling me off to the delivery room. Then I heard someone saying that I had delivered my baby. I felt my tummy before I believed it. My friend Marilyn had told me they would put a bracelet on me saying boy or girl. I couldn't read it so I said, "If I have had my baby, what is it?" When they said it was a little boy, I thought, "Well, that's not a girl."

I was remembering what Jim had said earlier in the labor room, that if it wasn't a girl, we were sending it back. That may seem insignificant, but as the story unfolds, you may see it in a different light.

James Duane Parton was born on May 23, 1963 in Dallas, Texas at 4:16 a.m. He weighed 6 pounds, 6 ounces, and was 19 inches long. Dr. Campbell came by the next morning and tweaking my toes said, "He's a little peanut, but he is all there." After all those months of waiting and hoping, it was wonderful to hear he was a perfect baby boy.

You can imagine the fear which overcame me when they brought him to me about 9:30 a.m. As I held him, he began to choke. Very foolishly, but naturally, I jumped out of bed to get help. Suddenly, I realized I might fall. I got back into the bed and called for a nurse. One came immediately. The nurse put her finger in his mouth and pulled out some birth phlegm. That was a normal situation but I didn't know it.

At last, I was able to lie with my darling baby boy in my arms and just bask in the joy and peace I felt as I looked at him. I had been able to carry him to full term, even though there had been some scary times. The delivery process had gone well. The two of us had done a fabulous job of getting him here. Oh, yes, the doctors and nurses helped too, but it was mostly Duane and me and God.

No one could have known then how he and I would have to struggle over and over to keep him safe and well.

My sister Ruth came to stay with us for a couple of weeks. My mother and stepfather visited us when Duane was a few weeks old. Those early weeks were about as expected with any newborn. However, he never did need as much sleep as I needed. Quite a lot of the early pictures show a rather sleepy mother.

I remember dedicating Duane to God when he was three weeks old. I thought I looked so pretty in my new little dress. Actually, I looked quite sleepy. Oh, well, we managed and I dearly loved being a stay-at-home mom.

Oh, I almost forgot to tell you that Sally and Dudley were Duane's Godparents. In fact, Jim and I drew up wills stating that if something should happen to both of us they would raise Duane.

Just a little interesting side thought. Duane is gone now, along with both Sally and Dudley, and here I am with the pleasure of being their two children's stepmother. I also have two wonderful granddaughters, Sarah and Rachel, through Stephanie (my stepdaughter) and her husband, Zenon. My stepson Mike and his wife Jennifer make our family complete. Throughout the rest of the book I will refer to them as my children (omitting the word "step"). They are all so special to me and I am very blessed that they care about me.

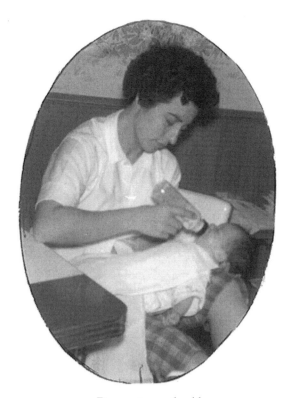

Duane at 2 weeks old

As I think back on Duane's life, his sweet, sensitive nature was apparent very early. My friend, Marilyn, and I loved to have coffee together in the mornings. Mostly I went to her home, because she had two children and I had only Duane. We used to put Duane and Darren in the playpen together. Even though they were almost the same age, Darren was quite a bit larger. He was rough with Duane, but Duane would never fight back. Once Darren bit Duane and left teeth marks on his back, which he carried as long as he lived.

Duane never did like to fight. He used to tell me the other kids were picking on him and I said, "Well, if they hit you, just hit them back." That kind of retaliation seemed to work when I was a kid. However, Duane just could never take up for himself. Perhaps I was wrong. I thought if I tried to settle his disagreements, the other children would really pick on him.

Once, Duane did try to defend himself. He told me about it during the last couple of weeks of his life. We did a lot of talking during that time. He told me about a fight he had when he was in elementary school. The one time he hit a boy, who had been picking on him, he knocked out a tooth. After the fight, one of the teachers put boxing gloves on both boys, and put them in the ring. Unfortunately, the other boy was much bigger than Duane and used to fighting. He beat Duane up pretty badly. The other kids kept telling Duane not to get up, but he would not stay down.

I am not sure what ended the fight or how I could not have seen his injuries. When Duane told me about it, I was ready to fight! I tried to get him to tell me who the teacher was, so I could find him and give him a piece of my fist or at least my mouth. Laughing, Duane said, "Oh, Mother, that was 25 years ago. It is okay. Let it go."

I don't think careless fighting is good, but without a fighting spirit, I think life would have defeated me long ago. No, I don't go around hitting people as an adult, but don't pick on my family or you will deal with me.

I guess I got my fighting spirit from both my parents. They were wonderful and even though my daddy died when I was 12 years old, he taught me a lot. Once when my cousin's leg was broken, her mother stood screaming, "I can't stand it, I can't stand it." My daddy took her by the shoulders and shaking her said, "Shut up, by God you will stand it." After Daddy's death, Mother, my little brother, Robert, who was 10, and I were a little family within the larger family. Like Daddy, Mother was protective of us.

Even though Duane's sweet, gentle spirit never wanted to fight others; he did inherit the same fighting spirit for life. That was one of the characteristics Dudley loved the most about Duane.

Dudley, or "Uncle Dud", as Duane called him, was in and out of Duane's entire life. Duane was fine with church as a baby, but by the time he was a few months old, he started crying when we got near the church. To make things worse, Dudley would tease him. I was young, so was Dud, and I didn't know then that I could have said, "Don't do that."

Well, as life would have it, we got a miracle. A woman named Ms. Mackey came into our lives. The first Sunday she worked at the church, she took Duane up in her arms and said, "Look out the window at the birds."

That was the end of Duane's church trauma. In fact, for many years, she was not only Duane's babysitter, but also took care of Sally and Dudley's children, Stephanie and Michael.

You can see how intertwined our lives were. Recently, I looked through some old pictures. Sure enough, in the early years, Stephanie and Michael were always there in Duane's birthday party pictures.

People sometimes ask me if I had been given any clues that Duane was homosexual. I really don't know. I didn't pick up on them if they were there. As I said to the young woman, Shahn, who was Duane's therapist the last two years of his life, "Duane and I never had a chance." When I was about 16, some students said one of our teachers might be gay. Truly, I didn't know what a homosexual was then. To top it off, talk about politically incorrect, they were called "queers." How unkind, but no worse than the names my son was called when he was just in the third or fourth grade.

You may wonder what rock I grew up under. It was a normal small town in Northeastern Oklahoma. I was one of the more innocent ones. I grew up in a wonderful Methodist Church and simply didn't read improper literature. I always wanted to please my mother and Jesus. That is right; Jesus was as real to me as my parents. My loyalty to Him was not out of fear, but love.

I didn't have a point of reference when Duane was young. I just saw this loving, happy, sensitive boy as the wonderful child that he was. He played with trucks, liked little girls, and climbed on his swing set. In fact, once when he was about two years old, he climbed up the ladder to come down the slide. However, he suddenly decided he would walk across the top pipe that holds the swings and slide together. Of course, I was horrified! Somehow I knew if I shouted at him, he would step out there and fall. I said, "Let's talk about this." I don't know how long it took, but I convinced him it would be a good idea to come down the slide.

I certainly didn't see Duane as a sissy, but a rather sensitive child. He was kind and gentle; isn't that what women say they want in their men and often don't get?

Duane and I had a very special day together in the park before our lives changed forever. The doctor had discovered I had a huge cyst the size of a grapefruit in my abdomen. He did not think it was malignant, but it was scary for me.

My daddy had died at age 46 from cancer and my mother's sister from ovarian cancer. That meant I was at risk from both sides of my family. I was trying to be brave because that was what I had been taught to be. I was 33 years old and Duane was seven. I knew there was a possibility I might die.

I wanted to take Duane to the park by myself and have that special picture in my mind. We had such a good time. I told my mother, who had come to be with me, that if I died, I didn't want people to be sad and say how young I was. I said, "I have experienced every kind of love there is. My parents and siblings have loved me, as well as my mother-in-law and father-in-law. I have known the great love of my husband

and my precious little boy. I have had it all." I felt so blessed and I was.

It was a very difficult and extensive surgery, a complete hysterectomy. It was a slow recovery, but I had lots of support. Fortunately, the mass was benign and I didn't die. God allowed me to live to be here for Duane.

Unfortunately, my world fell apart soon after the surgery. Jim had found someone else. He left our home when Duane was seven and a half. I knew Duane was young, but as I look back, he was still just a baby.

Perhaps this is the place to say that this book is not about bashing Duane's father for leaving us. Nor is it about all the mistakes I made which I will reveal as we go along.

My hope is that everyone who reads this book will realize this is a book about love. In fact, it is about extreme love; unconditional love; love that surpasses what many people ever feel. It is not only about my love for my son, but his love for me. Truly he and I were blessed to experience this kind of forgiving, supporting, long-suffering love.

Now, please read on to see if there are lessons, or perhaps I should say ideas, you can use in your life. Maybe, just maybe, there is someone in your life who needs this kind of unconditional love. Yes, we had our differences, but as Duane once said when he was about 33, "Mother, we often disagree in theory, but we almost always agree in specific cases." This was so true.

I can remember the day I first saw something in Duane that concerned me. I saw him walk across our large den and start down the hall to his room. I thought, "He looks just like me." That troubled me. I am sure I didn't handle the situation as I should have. Jim had remarried immediately after our divorce. His new wife, Liz, and I had worked together and I had thought we were friends, so I really believed I could go talk to them.

Mistakenly, I went to their home without calling–bad idea. I told them what I had observed and said that he needed some male influence. As you might expect, I wasn't received very well. It was then that I realized that I was on my own as far as parenting Duane.

What hurt the most was that Liz had three little girls his daddy was raising and loving. Duane did have a relationship later with at least one of the girls and her husband.

His father was not a bad person, just absent most of the time. He was never late with a child support check for which I was grateful. However, writing a check is the easiest part of being a parent. Giving a child time, whether we live with them or in another house, is the hard work.

No, this is not about blame. I introduced too many men into Duane's life. People often ask me if I am sorry I married Duane's father. Of course, I am not. We had 15 wonderful years together. Why did he leave us then? I could never get an answer from him. I have some theories, but that is all they are. That is perhaps important to me, but not to Duane's story. What is important is that Duane felt abandoned by his father.

The year before he died, I was rubbing his back to ease some pain he was having. Duane said, "You know, Mother, I think I was born with a propensity towards men, but I think I have been looking for my Dad's love all my life."

I wanted to scream, "I've been trying to tell you that ever since you were 16." I didn't say those words. It was too late. I just replied, "I think you are probably right son."

Physically speaking, life with Duane was always a little challenging. He was about six months old when President Kennedy was shot. In fact, I had just come inside from hanging out diapers on the clothesline (yes, we really did that) when my friend Marilyn called to tell me about our President. That, of course, was devastating to all of us.

It was about this time that Duane developed croup. He was so sick his doctor offered to make a house call at night if needed, even though they had stopped house calls by then. He told me to make a tent over his crib with a sheet. I was to place a vaporizer under the tent to keep his lungs hydrated. Well, I nearly steamed the little fellow to death. It really was hard to raise children without grandparents but many of us were doing that. We did the best we could.

When he was about two years old we had a very unusual spiritual experience. Duane was running a rather high fever. I had done all the things the doctor said to do and he was still so hot. He was lying on his bed and I was sitting beside him. I was alone and very frightened. I didn't know what to do.

Today I would tell my daughter to take a little one to the emergency room. Back then we didn't do that very much. At that time I had never heard anyone pray for a miracle healing, so what I did was just instinctive. I put my hand on his chest and said, "In the name of Jesus, I command this fever to come out of my baby's body." Immediately, I felt his little chest cool under my hand. All at once it seemed there was a wind inside my head and Duane and I were being lifted up in a wind. Then there was this calm, peaceful feeling that swept over me. I really didn't know my Bible that well, but I remembered the Holy Spirit coming like a wind to the disciples in the Upper Room.

I knew I had just experienced a miracle. I know now, it was not Duane's time to die. If you are not a believer in Jesus and the Bible, please don't put down this book. I am simply telling the story of my darling boy's life.

Then there was the time he got his hand under the lawn mower, clipped off the tip edge of one finger, and mangled two other tips pretty badly. He was probably about 13 years old. In the ER Duane didn't want me to look at his hand. We waited awhile for the doctor. He asked me to read to him. When they took him for X-rays, they propped his hand up and I saw how awful his fingers looked. They looked like shredded carrots. Duane was so brave during this time. He even opened the door for me when we left the hospital that day.

Of course, it was his right hand that was injured, which was his writing hand. He never missed a day of school and continued making wonderful grades.

By the time of this accident, I had been introduced to Bill Coats and his aloe plant products. Using them on the sly, as the doctor didn't believe in them, we did a great job of healing his fingers. Only the clipped finger showed something had happened. Duane was glad he had something to show for that awful accident.

We laughed about it later, but there was nothing funny about it that day. Our lives were truly "constant adventures."

There were other injuries, too numerous to name. Another really serious one happened when he was in high school. He was working at a restaurant. As he pushed a trash bag in the dumpster, a piece of glass cut his hand and blood went everywhere. They called me to go directly to the hospital. I can still see the blood splattered exam room. Again, there was no complaining.

To have had such a gentle spirit, Duane was very brave about accidents. I suppose they each served to build into Duane an indomitable spirit. He needed that spirit desperately those last six years of his life as he lived with Aids.

Did you catch the wording? Duane always said, "I am not dying from a fatal disease. I am living with a life threatening disease." Pretty neat attitude, wouldn't you say?

CHAPTER 2

Duane's Coming-Out Party

* * *

One of the worst nights of my life was the night Duane told me that he was gay. He was either 15 or 16. I guess there would never have been a good time for me to hear what I considered bad news. I had feared this might happen, but kept praying I was imagining things. I was working at my desk on my income tax, trying to complete the information for my CPA when Duane came to tell me he was going out. In addition our company convention was being held that weekend.

He had on a pair of sunglasses that hid his eyes. I said something about not liking his glasses because I could not see his eyes. He said that with them, he could hide from the world. I asked, "Do you have something to hide?" Pausing, he said he wanted to talk to me. I said to give me a minute as he walked into his room.

Entering his room I had no idea what a defining moment this was going to be for both of us. I sat down on his bed. He took hold of both my hands by lacing his fingers through mine and pushed me down on the bed with him seated at my side. As he told me his news, he bent back my fingers until I thought he was going to break every one of them. I don't remember all he said, but I do remember him saying, "I can't hide this from you any longer."

His friends had told him not to tell me, but he and I were so close that he didn't want this secret to be between us. I didn't say much of anything. I suppose I was in shock and my heart was breaking into a million pieces as he spoke. After a few minutes, he did go out for the evening.

You might ask why this was so hard for both of us. We had both read the Bible and knew what it said about homosexuality. We also both knew how hard it is to say "no" to the natural sexual desires we have.

Now, before you all go crazy on me, I am not saying the gay lifestyle is all about sex any more than the heterosexual life is all about sex. We all do have to admit that the expression of our sexual desires is the way we express our deepest love. Yes, sometimes it is sex for the sake of sex or lust as some would say. For many of us, it is a search for love. Granted, it is the wrong way to search for love, but it is, oh, so common.

After Duane left that night, I cried and cried and then I cried some more. For those of you who have not experienced this, it is heartbreaking on so many levels.

My son was telling me that he was never going to have a marriage with children. I was never going to watch his handsome face looking at his bride as she came to him. I was never going to hold his babies. I was never going to look into that baby's eyes and see my son. The future I thought was going to happen for my wonderful son was not to be.

Since his daddy had left, I had worked so hard to give him a normal, happy life and all my efforts seemed to crumble before my very eyes. Of course, I questioned my parenting. What had I done wrong? What could I have done differently?

There was one man I had dated that I could have married, yet I walked away from him. He had a very gentle spirit and would have been a wonderful father to Duane. Would it have changed Duane's life? We will never know.

There was another man that I did marry and perhaps should not have. Although Bill and I were only married two years, I kept the name McKee. He and his family were gracious and continued welcoming Duane and me into all the family gatherings. Duane truly loved his Granny McKee. Once when Duane was in the hospital he wrote Bill a very sweet letter asking if he could call him dad. Bill answered that he would be honored.

Duane had often cried at night for his daddy. With every man I dated my first thought was, "Would he be a good husband and a good daddy to my little boy?"

I knew the craving of Duane's heart. I remember once when he was probably nine years old, he sat in the middle of my bed talking to me while I put on my makeup.

He said, "I am going to call my daddy and tell him he has a family on this side of the tracks too." I replied he shouldn't call because I had talked to his daddy and it hadn't worked. I said that once words are spoken you can't take them back. Who knows, maybe I should have let him call his daddy, and I am sure he called him when I didn't know anything about it.

Even now, all these years later, when I think of the night he told me he was gay, the tears come. After I had cried for some time, my mother called to visit. She could tell I had been crying. Of course, she asked why. I told her it was just something I was dealing with and that I was already thanking God for what I believed He would do.

Later that night when Duane came home, the shock had worn off a little and despair had set in. We tried to talk, but all I could do was cry. Years later he told me that my reaction had made him feel like a horrible person. Of course, I had not thought he was horrible, but that is how he felt. When we think of it, we know perception is reality. It makes me so sad when I think of how he must have felt.

We all just have to be more understanding of each other's feelings. Yet, we cannot control the way others feel or even how we feel. However, we must try not to let our feelings damage others or even ourselves.

The thing that was in our favor was that Duane and I were honest with each other. We did survive that night and many more. The glue that always held us together was this vast ocean of unconditional love we had for each other.

I mentioned my company was having a convention that weekend. Part of my family was in the business and came to Dallas to attend the convention. To this day, I have no idea how I pulled that night off, since not only was my family in the audience but my son who had just told me he was gay was ushering.

At the end of the evening my mother said, "Honey, I have never seen you look more beautiful than you did tonight when on stage." Talk about a miracle; that was one.

For years I did not talk about Duane's lifestyle. I kept praying God would lead him out of it. I thought the fewer people who knew about his behavior, the easier it would be for him to leave that life. I didn't just pray. I did everything I could to try to understand him. We talked ad nauseum. We struggled, we cried, usually holding each other; we both tried to listen.

I don't think a mother ever tried harder than I did to understand what her child was feeling. I went to a couple of gay bars with him and to a gay church. I know some of you are saying, "Go girl!" and others are saying, "How awful! How could you do such things?" I will tell you. I was desperate! I loved my child better than life. I would have died for him! I wanted him out of that lifestyle. I knew he wasn't happy. He put on a good front, but he certainly wasn't "gay," meaning happy and carefree.

How do I know so much about how Duane thought and felt? As I said before, he talked to me and talked to me and talked to me. WE BOTH STRUGGLED SO WITH THIS ISSUE. Yet we loved life and had some great times together.

If you can loosen up a bit about the whole matter, you may even see some humor in some of our struggles. The night I went to the gay church with him, they were serving communion. For those of you who aren't Christian, communion is very meaningful to those of us who love Jesus Christ as our Lord and Savior. We take communion in remembrance of His death on the cross for our sins. Our hearts are full of gratitude and love!

As I took communion that night I prayed, "Oh God, if this is a sin, please forgive me." I was very uptight about the entire experience, but God saw my heart. I believe He said, "It is okay my child. I love you and know you love your child and furthermore I love your child more than you do."

I am quite positive God loved me for trying so hard to relate to Duane. I do believe we serve a Lord that is much bigger than most of us can even begin to understand. I still think the acts and lifestyle of homosexuality are wrong according to the Bible, but I also know that God hates divorce and I have been divorced more than once. I am ashamed to admit that, but if I am not truthful with you and myself and most of all God, you can't trust anything I write.

People who are not believers can't understand that even as believers we still struggle with sin. We want to be perfect, we try to be perfect, we just can't be perfect. We are forgiven and the longer we are believers and develop a closer and closer walk with Christ, we hope we sin less. Old habits do not have quite the hold on us they once had. Christianity is not about dos and don'ts. It is a relationship with Jesus Christ.

It was hard to combat society. On television, homosexuality became a popular story line. It wasn't just acceptance of the lifestyle, but glorifying it. No matter how hard it was Duane and I hung in there together.

Although Duane said it wasn't true, I thought I had probably talked too much to Duane about the sinfulness of homosexual behavior instead of Jesus' acceptance of him and how He could help him resist his desires. At that time there wasn't much information available to a single mother who was raising a young boy with those desires. Remember, just a few years before, I didn't even know what a homosexual was.

I was in direct sales and I did a lot of evening meetings. I remember going to a Denny's restaurant one night after a meeting. A man I didn't know started getting fresh with me and frightened me. I said, "Excuse me while I speak to a friend of mine." I walked over to a policeman who was sitting at the end of the counter. I sat down by him and said quietly, "You are a friend of mine." He understood and went along with me. We had some really good conversation. I talked to him about Duane to get a man's perspective on it. He gave me good advice. He said not to try to be a mother and daddy to him. That would just confuse him. Just be the best mother I could be which is exactly what I was.

I sent Duane to talk to his Uncle Dud. I thought as a pastor he might take him under his wing and show him how to be a man. Instead, he just asked him how he felt about it. When Duane said he was okay with it, Dud said nothing more. Needless to say, I could have killed Dudley!

Yes, this is the same man I married years later after Sally died. In later years he was sorry he didn't try to help him. Back then most churches and ministers didn't want to confront us about any of our sins. That is sad because we really did need help looking at ourselves honestly...all of us.

Growing up, my mother told me all the time that she loved me, but she was also quick to point out my faults. Perhaps that is why I can see my sins as clearly as I do, although I am sure I am still blind to many of my sins and shortcomings.

I will tell you right now that my multiple marriages are a great embarrassment to me. I understand that God has forgiven me, but I don't want to be a bad example of a Christian. I am well aware of my sins. I suppose that is one reason I am so very grateful that I know Jesus as my Savior. When I speak publicly about my life, I confess that by the time I was eight years old, I knew I needed a Savior.

Duane was an excellent student. In fact, one of his early elementary teachers showed me some results of tests and said, "He is almost a genius." "How do I raise a genius?" I asked. She told me to remember that he was a little boy emotionally. It was fun raising such a lovable, bright little boy. We both loved going to church together. After his father left, staying in the church where we had worshipped was just too painful. We ended up joining the First Baptist Church of Richardson. Duane accepted Christ there. I knew that he understood what that meant because I was with him when the pastor talked to him about his decision. I had been baptized before, but the Baptist Church required me to be baptized again. Duane and I were baptized at the same time. We both loved sharing that special experience.

During his elementary years he did not relate well to his peers. As I just shared, he was brighter than most. Also, he was allergic to grass and dirt. When he tried to play ball and other outdoor sports, he would break out and his face would swell. So, while other boys were outside learning how to play ball, Duane was in the house reading encyclopedias.

When Duane was in about the fourth grade one of the school counselors called me into his office to discuss Duane's issues with his peers. I had never met the man and was a little nervous about meeting him.

Duane, at age 9, calling his grandmothers about his salvation experience

After visiting awhile he said, "I thought you might be Duane's problem. I thought you might be a smother mother, but I can see you are not." He went on to say that Duane was just too smart to relate to his peers, but that as he got older he would seek out people of his own intelligence and would do just fine. That is exactly what happened.

I was very proud of Duane. If he was with someone of normal intelligence, they never knew how bright he was. However, he could speak with the most intelligent people quite comfortably. He never had a superior attitude. He was such an exceptional person. I am so sorry his life was cut short. I still miss him every day.

No matter how I felt about Duane's lifestyle, I was always accepting of him as well as all his friends. When he was about 17, he came home late one afternoon and said a couple of boys he knew had just been thrown out of their homes because they had "come out" to their parents. He wanted me to let them stay with us.

Working as a sales manager had taught me to process a situation very quickly and make a decision. This was my thinking in this instance: If I let them stay with me, do I seem to be promoting this lifestyle? What about their parents? They had put them on the street. In those days there was a lot being said about tough love and maybe they thought they were doing the best thing. I, however, couldn't say that I followed Jesus Christ who loves all of us and tell my son they could not stay with us.

So, regardless of my beliefs about the lifestyle, I let them come into our home. It is hard to remember just how long they were there. I think it was a month or two. You can imagine the "Mother" talk I gave them. They were not supposed to do certain things in my home. Who knows what they did when I was gone, but they were all very respectful towards me. We had wonderful conversations and I hope they remember me as a kind, loving woman.

I recall one Sunday when I had come home from church to prepare lunch. I had a rather small, galley type kitchen. Just above my stove top was a bar that separated the dining room from the kitchen. I was frying chicken and they were all clustered around me. I mentally looked up to God and said, "Father, how did I get here?"

I'm sure many parents have had that same thought. For some it might be like my issue with Duane. For others it might be drugs, or kids that steal, or kids that lie, or girls that get pregnant out of wedlock. They are still our kids and I believe if God loves us in spite of our wrong doings, we must love our children. For Duane and me, not loving, was not an option.

Duane was more than a good student—he was an excellent student. He was a National Merit Scholar and went to Southern Methodist University primarily on scholarships. I helped him some and he also worked.

When people would ask him how he got all those scholarships, he would hold his arm out to his side and say, "Ever since I was this tall, mother told me I needed to make good grades so I could get scholarships for college, as she did not have enough money to pay all my expenses."

We were blessed. I did work hard and kept us in a nice home and I was able to drive a good car. His dad helped him a time or two with cars. We had a good life; a very fun and rewarding life.

Duane was active in the local DeMolay organization. While participating, he received many awards, one of which had not been presented to anyone in his chapter for many years.

Duane was also active in the Junior Achievement program. When he was a junior in high school he said, "You might want to come to this meeting, I might get an award." He didn't make it sound like a big deal, but the recognition included most all the metroplex schools; Dallas, Richardson, Garland, Plano, Irving, and perhaps others. Well, was I ever thrilled when he received President of the Year!

The next year when the awards banquet was held, my company was having their convention. There was a reception for us right across the street from Duane's banquet. I told my boss I would be a little late as I had to go be a momma. He totally understood.

Duane really didn't expect to win President of the Year again, as he was in competition with two very smart girls who happened to be his friends. When the presenter said, "We have never had anyone receive this award two years in a row before," my heart jumped straight up into my throat. Then he said, "The President of the Year is Duane Parton."

I jumped up and without knowing I was going to, I cried out, "That's my son!" In times past Duane might have been embarrassed as I waved my hands in the air, but he was so thrilled that I was excited! There were many times he made me proud of him and this was certainly one of them.

Duane came back home one summer while he was in college and it did not go well. I remember once he said not to mother him so. I really don't remember my offense. I said, "Well, I know how to be your mother. If you want me to be something different, you will have to tell me what you want." After thinking about it a few minutes, he decided I should just be his mother. As I recall, he stayed a few weeks, and then made other arrangements.

As you would expect, Duane did excellently at SMU. He received several awards while there. During that time, he and an older man moved in together. One night they took me to the Majestic to see the "Tuna," and later to dinner. They sat on one side of the booth and I was on the other side.

Later, Duane told me they weren't just friends. I said I suspected as much. He said, "If you had asked me to choose between you two, Mother, I would have chosen my friend." You can imagine how that hurt.

No parent wants to hear those words, but we know that as our children grow, it is natural for someone to come into their lives that will be first before us. Many an in-law gets in trouble over that reality. Most of us just don't expect to be an in-law to a gay couple. No matter the pain, again, my love for him won out.

In 1985 I sold my house and bought another one. I made some money on the deal, so I told Duane that I would take him on a vacation to celebrate his graduation from SMU. Over the years I had paid for Duane to attend JA jamborees, DeMolay functions, and church camps, but he and I had not had a vacation since his daddy left. We talked about where we might go. One day he saw a budget I had for my profit on the house. He said, "Oh, I didn't know we had that much for vacation." Of course I told him we didn't have to spend all that money. He said he wanted us to take an American Express Tour to Europe. We got tour books and we looked at them (mostly he looked). He was very detail oriented, so he figured exactly how much money we would need.

To make a long story short–we toured Europe! We thought it was the highlight of both our lives. This may surprise you, but actually the last two weeks of his life and his death were in many ways the highlight of our time together.

Throughout his college years, Duane came home a lot on Saturdays and just hung out with me. One of his favorite things for me to do was make nachos. I made them on a large platter and we ate right off the platter together. We laughed and talked. Oh, yes, how we talked, all of his life. We talked about everything. I have often told people that I can tell them more about homosexuality than they want to know. Some of the talk was very painful, but I am not sorry we talked. However, most of our talks were fun.

College Years

As I write, a funny story comes to my mind. One evening I was at my desk at home when I had a very bad chest pain. It didn't run down my arm, so I didn't actually think it was my heart, but I thought I should call someone. At that time, Duane lived only a few miles away, so I called and said, "Son, I am having a pretty bad pain in my chest. Will you call me back in about 15 or 20 minutes? If I don't answer, please come see about me." He assured me that he would.

Well, I didn't die, or even have a heart attack. I waited for an hour and called him back. When he heard my voice, he said, "Oh, Mother, I am so sorry! The time got away from me. Are you okay?" Once he knew, yes, I was okay, we both laughed and of course he felt badly that he had forgotten me.

The moral to this story is, if you are having a chest pain, call 911 or at least a neighbor who can come sit with you. As a matter of fact, I did just that a few months ago. I called my friend, Linda, and she came and sat with me for about an hour.

Duane and I loved to shop together. He was the better shopper. He could find a bargain where there wasn't one. He told me I could shop at Neiman-Marcus. I just had to wait for "Last Call." On one of our excursions, I bought one of the very first (I think) Vera Wang dresses. I was slender then and I wore that dress a lot. It was a perfect business banquet dress, meeting dress, and yes, even church dress.

One shopping day that I will always hold dear to my heart was a Saturday. I suppose Duane was about 19 or 20 at the time. He came over and I asked, "How would you like to drive to Salado?" This quaint little town is a couple of hours south of Dallas. We talked the whole trip. I don't remember what I bought him, but I got a gorgeous Christmas tree skirt which I still use.

Another day, we were driving and he said, "If I ever found a girl who loved me as much as you do, I would marry her." During the last week of his life he mentioned a particular girl and said, "I should have married her. She would have been an excellent wife and we could have been happy." What can I say? I certainly made my share of mistakes too.

Duane loved to reach over and hold my hand as we drove together. It's possible that when he was two or three years old, he should have disconnected from me and bonded with his father. There are some people who believe that little boys who do not shift their main bond from mother to father sometimes fall into homosexuality.

CHAPTER 3
Decisions—Right or Wrong

* * *

    This book is not an attempt to give reasons for or against the gay lifestyle. This is a book to honor the love between a mother and son and later to honor my son for the way he lived with AIDS. However, it also shows the results of wrong decisions. His father and I made some wrong decisions and Duane made some. The result was that he had some very turbulent times and his life ended much too soon. Let me clarify something for you. When I say Duane's father made wrong decisions, I am not saying it was wrong for him to leave our home. I just wish he would have included Duane in his life more.

    I have always believed that parenting is one job that you don't really know how you are doing until it is too late. There were hints along the way, but at the end of this book, you will discover that I did more right than wrong. If you will give your children unconditional love, you can make a lot of mistakes and still win in the game of life.

    More on our trip to Europe…we flew to New York City, then on to Amsterdam. In New York we met a girl and her mother whom we spent a lot of time with on the tour. The girl had graduated from high school and was quite taken with Duane and he liked her as well. Their friendship made for a very nice tour. We were with a group of about 40 or 50 people. We visited Innsbruck, Austria; Mannheim, Germany; Rome, Venice, and Milan, Italy; Geneva, Switzerland; Paris, France; and London, England. By the way, if any of our fellow travelers read this book, I would love to hear from you.

We had a glorious time. The trip was paid in full before we departed. However, we spent so much on shopping (what else?) that when we got to the Duty Free shop in London, I said, "Don't look to the right or the left. We have spent everything, even my money market." We took this trip the last of July and first of August 1985. The next April or May the company I worked for was sold and I lost my great job.

People asked, "Aren't you sorry you spent all that money on your trip?" I said I absolutely was not sorry. I felt that if I stayed healthy I would make money again.

We took rolls and rolls of pictures. I made double prints so he wouldn't have to wait until I died to have the pictures. Who knew then he would die before me? People told me I couldn't get good pictures through the bus windows, but I did.

At Duane's service after his death, the pastor (who knows and loves me) said, "Duane was very strong-willed. Wonder where he gets that trait?" Okay, I know. I believe I am a reasonable person, but yes, I am very strong-willed. Life would have crushed me long ago if I hadn't been strong.

Duane once said, "Mother, I thank you so much for taking me to Europe. I didn't just see the world; I became a part of it." I guess that is one reason we loved to do things for each other and give gifts to each other. We were both so appreciative of what the other did for us.

Decisions–Right or Wrong

Duane and Elaine in London

Duane received his B.A. in English in May 1985 and his B.A. in Business that December. That May I had an open house honoring him in my new home. We had quite a gathering for Duane and he loved it.

He was hired as a purchasing agent right out of college with Sanger-Harris which later became Foley's. He was transferred to Houston and worked with them until 1992. Duane knew my style and what flattered me. From time to time, he would send me a surprise. One day I opened a package from him to see this gorgeous cobalt blue long leather coat with a black fox fur collar. Wow! Was it ever beautiful!

When Duane told me this story, it made the coat even more special. He walked into work one day and saw this coat hanging on a rack before him. He said, "That coat is my mother's!" Then he looked at the price and said, "Oh, I guess it isn't." Not long after, he walked by the rack again and saw that it was on sale. When he looked at the price, he said, "I knew that was my mother's!" Isn't that a fun and sweet story?

A special gift–A fox fur windshield scraper

Can you get a feel for our love for each other? I want to encourage all of you to reach out to someone and show them this kind of unconditional love. Now we all know it is easy to love those who agree with us about everything, but how about reaching out to someone who does not see things as you do? I promise you, it is worth the effort. There is no amount of money that I would take for what Duane and I had. I am just grateful that we had 35 years. What an honor to be his Mom!

About this time, I had a life changing experience. I met a young man at my church, who had just been diagnosed with AIDS. He had asked for prayer for cancer. God just whispered in my ear that he had AIDS. This disease was fairly new and there was a lot of fear about it.

I stopped him as he left the church to tell him about a support line that he could call night or day. I also gave him my phone number and said to feel free to call me. He called that night, then the next night. On the third night he said, "You have been so nice to me. I have to tell you. I don't have cancer. I have AIDS."

I told him God had revealed that to me. He said, "Would you have quizzed me until I told you?" I asked, "Did I?" Then I told him that I thought we all have a deep inner core where no one has a right to go unless we invite them there.

We became fast friends. We sat together in church; we ate together, and went to concerts in the park. We talked every day. We had several months where we shared deep feelings, including his fears and hopes.

He and Duane and I attended church on Easter that year. Duane gave me a beautiful cross with opals on the tips of the cross and an aquamarine stone in the middle. So you see, even when he didn't always want me to talk to him about my faith, he always honored my faith.

Later that year, the young man was in the hospital nine days and nights and I stayed with him all that time, except for a brief trip home for clothes. I was gone about two or three hours. When I got back to the hospital he said, "There has sure been a lot of water go over the dam since you left." I never left him again. He had made peace with God before he died.

Once, during the middle of the night, I was so tired. I decided I would go lie down for a few minutes in the family room. As I walked out into the hallway, I saw the sign for the chapel. All at once, without planning to do so, I found myself going into the chapel. It was so quiet and peaceful. I had never really worshipped routinely in a church where I raised my hands. However, there, in the presence of our Holy God, I raised my hands to the Father and began to softly sing praises to God. I learned something that night. When we are in deep pain or sorrow, if we will just get our minds and hearts off ourselves and focus on Jesus, miraculous things happen. I don't really know how long I worshipped God, but at some point I realized I felt rested and renewed. Without sleeping, I went back to my friend and to my vigil of love.

Another time, I stood watching him sleep and I thought, "If I had not gone to church the night I met my friend, I would not be here. God loved him so much, He would have provided someone else for this sweet boy, but I do believe I was God's first choice. If I had not been obedient, I would have missed this blessing."

I am sure I saw my friend enter Heaven. It was sometime around 3:00 a.m. I happened to be alone with him. He had asked me to hold his hand. He had been in a deep sleep for some time. We thought it was nearing his time to leave us to go to Jesus. I gently laid my hand on his.

All at once, I saw this bright light and two figures were standing in the center of it in white robes. I couldn't see their faces, but I knew it was Jesus and my friend. Voices rang out, "Enter into His gates with thanksgiving and into His courts with praise!" Simultaneously, two thoughts went through my brain. First, I thought, "Jesus stood to receive my friend like He stood when Stephen (the first martyr) was dying! What love Jesus had for this young man!" My second thought was, "Those words sounded like a Psalm. Sure enough, they are the beginning words of Psalm 100:4 (KJV)."

What a glorious experience that was! Truly how blessed I was through this friendship. How I loved this boy. He had struggled with his feelings, but he and God won in the end.

By the way, his parents were at the hospital in the family room. It was just very hard on them to be with him constantly because they had no warning. They really didn't know he was gay until he got sick. I'm glad I could be there for the family as well as my friend. This also helped prepare me for what I was going to have to deal with when Duane became ill.

Duane said, "Mother I didn't think you knew what you were getting into when you became his friend. I didn't know if you could see it through to the end. I do think God let you see him enter Heaven as a reward for your faithfulness to him. I'm very proud of you."

Before dying, my friend said, "God is going to bless you for this Sweetheart. (Yes, that is what he called me.) It may be great, it may be small, but it will be an unbelievable blessing." This was a wonderful experience in itself. I have had so many blessings since then, but I really feel there are more to come. My prayer is that this book will bless people, even though there are some tough subjects discussed in it.

It seems that often after a spiritual high like this, we get "sucker punched." At Thanksgiving, my niece, Sandy, whom I had not seen for several years was going to be at my mother's home. Everyone was coming in for the family gathering. When I told Mother that I was so excited about seeing everyone, she told me she didn't think the family would want me around since I had been with that boy who had AIDS.

I was crushed. I told her that I had not kissed him on the mouth or had sex with him and that I had worn gloves when he was in the hospital. She didn't budge.

So, I called my sister Evelyn. I thought Mother was just getting older and didn't understand. Evelyn's response was,

"Well, we can't have anything controversial." I couldn't believe it! I was not going to get to see my niece.

Sometime later I realized that if God was going to give me a ministry to young gay men, and it seemed He was, I needed to know what it feels like to be rejected by one's family.

As I contemplate all this, I realize I have experienced a lot of rejection in my lifetime. The one constant has always been God. He has always been there with outstretched arms saying, "Come to me and let me hold you and soothe away all your hurts. I love you unconditionally, now and forever." He wants to do the same for you.

I don't want to seem like Miss Goody Two-Shoes. Rarely, but yes, on an occasion I could be a little naughty. After being told I couldn't go home for Thanksgiving, Mother said my brother had talked to a doctor in his Bible group, who said that if I wore gloves, I was probably safe. Mother invited me up for Christmas.

I said, "No, if I wasn't good enough to come Thanksgiving, I'm not coming Christmas." Okay, so I am not a saint! You don't really want me to be one do you? After all, this book is about trying to write the truth as it was, not as I wished life could have been. I hope I am giving you permission to look at your flaws. Just remember God loves you and will help you change your behavior, if you want Him to do so. He and I are always working on me. I like to say that when I feel I have one fault under a little better control, God holds up a mirror to my heart and says, "Look, my sweet girl, see this dirty spot over here in your heart. We are going to work on that next. Remember though, I am with you always. I will help you in your struggles."

After being single for 12 years, I married again in 1988. I met Jack in church and even though I realized he was a good ole' country boy, and I was a city girl, I thought we could make it. He said all the things I wanted to hear. It was not a wise marriage, but there were some really good times. Jack and I moved to his small farm a couple of hours north of Dallas where I lived for about four years. As one friend said, those were some of my best years and some of my worst years. I developed some precious relationships that live on until today.

During this time, Duane was in Houston and I was traveling with my job, so I didn't see him much, but talked to him often by phone. Our relationship was pretty steady, although we did have a few tense moments. One Christmas he brought his male friend, Larry, to the farm. While discussing arrangements, I told him I wanted Larry to come because I loved him, too. However, in my home, they could not sleep together. He replied, "Oh, Mother."

You all know that tone. I explained that when I visited them in their apartment, I accepted the fact they went off to their bedroom at night. However, in my home, they had to accept my rules. I went on to say that I would not allow him to bring a girl home to sleep with either if they were not married.

Even if you don't agree with me, you will see that it worked out for the best in the long run. I am not asking for you to agree with me. This is our story, not yours. Our issue was homosexuality. You may have a different issue with someone you love. I pray something I have experienced will give you strength and hope as you show unconditional love towards someone else. And if you are struggling, I hope you will find a way to change a behavior you have that is causing you hurt and pain. Perhaps you need to ask someone to love you in spite of your issues. I pray you will feel God's love for you.

In early 1991 Duane was shot on the streets of Houston. He was walking from a friend's apartment back to his own apartment when two boys started chasing him. They yelled "stop" but he didn't.

When he kept running, one of them shot him. Duane said he heard a zing and he fell forward, sliding his hands on the debris on the street. His hands were pretty roughed up. The boys came up behind him and took his wallet out of his back pocket. The shooter asked if he had money in his front pockets. He said, "Yes sir." Then they turned him over and went through his front pockets. There was no one around and he was pretty sure they were going to kill him. Duane said he was thinking, "You were a coward to shoot me from behind, but if you kill me, you are going to have to do it looking into my eyes." He said he fixed his eyes on the boy's eyes with the gun and never blinked.

I have heard that you shouldn't stare at these kinds of men; that they take it as a challenge, but it may have saved his life. He also thanked me for teaching him to be polite. He supposed the boy had never been called "Sir" before. That may have been part of why they didn't shoot him. They told him not to get up until they were out of sight. He didn't.

God was with him in so many ways that night. He had good insurance and had been to the doctor several times in the last few weeks. He had memorized his insurance ID number. He was bleeding pretty badly but was able to get to a public phone about three blocks away. He called 911 and was able to give them his name and location. Then he passed out.

A policeman found him and stayed with him until the ambulance came. He was dressed in jeans and a cowboy shirt. He said, "I sure didn't look like a successful executive for Foley's." He came to and gave them his name and insurance ID number. Otherwise they would have taken him to the county hospital. He passed out on the way to the hospital, but regained consciousness again when he needed to give his admitting information.

The bullet had gone into the back of his leg just above his right knee. It traveled up the leg and came out one inch below his right testicle. No major arteries were hit. No major lasting damage. They kept him in the hospital overnight just to be sure no clots formed or other complications occurred.

Duane said he learned something important that night. He found out how much he really wanted to live. He knew he could have laid there and bled to death. That was not what he wanted. In fact, he worked very hard to live.

When Duane called and told me about what had happened, I said, "Thank God. Some little grandma had been praying for her grandson. Had he killed you, I would have awakened that day without my son and that boy would have awakened a murderer."

Mothers and grandmas often have a way of knowing when their kids are in trouble. They don't always know what they are doing, but they just know their kids aren't living as they should.

So many times people think they are doing just fine without God. They have no idea how many prayers are being lifted to God on their behalf.

That reminds me of a time when Duane was just out of college. This was a period when he wasn't so antagonistic about God. He called me and asked me to pray for a friend of his who was going for an interview later that week. I said of course that I would. We visited a little more then I asked, "Now on which day am I supposed to pray, Wednesday or Thursday?" Then I laughed and said, "Well, I guess it wouldn't hurt me to pray for two days. And, if you are really nice, I might even throw in a prayer for you." He quickly replied, "Well, I figure you pray for me every day anyway." What confidence he had in me and in my love for him. He was always sure of how much I loved him and wanted the best for him.

A short time after Duane was shot, I was talking to him and he said his roommate wanted him to go out. He said, "I told him I was on medication. I couldn't go out drinking and coking."

I didn't know anything about drugs, but I asked with great feeling and mystery in my voice, "Are you talking about cocaine?"

He said, "Oh Mother (there it is again, that tone), it is just recreational. We have had this conversation before."

"No, son," I replied, "this is not a conversation I would have forgotten." This was the first time I had any idea he used drugs. He had been so against that in high school.

After all this time, it is still very difficult for me to tell you what Duane told me about that night he got shot. Sometime during the last year of his life, he told me the complete truth about what happened.

He said, "Mother, drugs will make you do lots of things you don't think you would ever do. The night I got shot, I was actually walking the street hoping to be picked up and paid for sexual favors."

My precious son, a prostitute! Yes, he hoped to sell his body for money to buy drugs. Once more, I thought my heart would break into a million pieces. I thanked Duane for telling me the truth and told him how grateful I was that he was not killed that night.

Most parents never hear all these stories. Even though all these things hurt deeply and I cry as I write about them, I am so glad Duane trusted our love enough to confide in me.

When I speak to the offenders in prison, I tell them I not only have Duane's permission to tell his story, but he really gave me a mandate to tell it.

You see, just three weeks before he died, I was in his home in Houston. He was sitting at his computer in his undershorts. By this stage, he had problems with his bowels, so often he just wore his shorts around the apartment. As I looked at him, a wave of deep, deep love and compassion swept over me. I asked, "Son, I have seen you sitting there so many times, may I take your picture?"

He answered immediately, with no hesitation, "Sure Mother." Then he stood and said, "Here, take one of me and my pain pole." Then he picked up a leg brace lying nearby and said, "Take this one too, Mother. I want you to go educate the world!"

When Duane told me that, he knew what I was going to say. He knew I would say that homosexuality is not compatible with Biblical teachings; but that I loved him more than life and that I had always given him unconditional love.

I not only loved him, but loved his friends. A few of them still stay in touch with me. I am hoping that I will hear from lots of people who knew Duane when they read his story. Actually, it is "our story."

I can just hear him now cheering me on, saying, "Come on, Mother. Don't cry. You can do this. I know you can. The world needs to hear the good news our love brings; the hope for them and their loved ones."

Stay with me, those of you who are reading this. We win! God brings victory out of such pain and sorrow. Hang in here with me. I know some of this is difficult to read. Just think how difficult it was for Duane and me to live it. Please don't forget, we always had fun even in the midst of our pain!

Once, years before, I told Duane that I would probably speak about all this after he was gone. His reply was, "Why are you waiting? Go ahead Mother and tell people about us now."

I took his advice and started telling our story to different classes and groups at Lovers Lane United Methodist Church where my husband, Dudley Dancer, was the Senior Associate. Duane was very pleased because he knew I spoke about our love as well as the fact that I wanted him out of that lifestyle.

Once he said, "Mother, when you stand up as the preacher's wife and talk about your gay son who has AIDS, you give everyone permission to talk about whatever their problem is."

He was right. Many people have shared their heartaches with me. They sense I am a safe place to be real, since I am so real about our struggles.

All my life, people have said how loving I am. I just thought that was my personality. Just in the last couple of years, I have realized that, yes, maybe a tiny bit of it is the way I was designed, but mostly it is God's unconditional love flowing through me to others. That is what people feel, God's unconditional love! How amazing and humbling that He would allow us to be a part of spreading His love around the world.

The year 1991 holds another very strong memory for me. One Sunday morning as I was preparing for church, I read a scripture card which was stuck up on my bathroom mirror. It was from John 6:37. It says, "All that my Father has given Me shall come to Me and he that cometh to Me I will in no wise cast out" (paraphrased).

Always before, I thought how wonderful that Jesus didn't cast out those that come. That day I saw "shall come to Me" and I thought, that's right, God. You gave Duane to Jesus when he was a little boy and I could hear…"Duane, Duane, Duane," ringing in my ears. I knew then that God would be faithful and that Duane would return to his belief in Jesus Christ.

I don't really think Duane ever totally gave up his belief in Jesus, but he knew what the Bible said about homosexuality and he didn't know what to do about his feelings. It was just easier to say he didn't believe than to try to reconcile his feelings with what he knew God said about that lifestyle.

It's like my sweet Dudley used to say about various things from the Bible, "I wish Jesus hadn't said that." It is difficult for all of us to give up something that feels so much like us. For instance, have you spoken with an alcoholic lately? They are born with certain genes and yet, if they don't want to destroy their lives, they must give up alcohol…totally.

Thankfully, there are now a few organizations, which are available to people who want to give up the gay lifestyle. They may or may not be able to walk away from their feelings, but they can leave the behavior. I don't know if I had those desires if I could overcome them, so I believe we should be very patient with those who struggle with these feelings.

When I speak in prison on the power of prayer, I tell them that sometimes God says yes, sometimes He says no, and often He says wait. God promised me in 1991 that Duane would return to his belief not only in God, but also in Jesus as his Savior.

I had to wait until January of 1998 for that prayer to be answered with a resounding "yes!"

I would like to tell you that my faith never wavered, but that would not be true. Most of the time I did believe, but we had a couple of rough years in which I sometimes thought, "Is that really what God was saying to me?" Then I would remember back to that moment and hear those words, "all (*not some*) that my Father has given me shall (*not maybe*) come to me." Once again, my faith would be strengthened, and I would hang onto God's word and believe.

The year of 1991 was very emotional for me. I lost my job when my employer replaced me with someone else he had known for a long time. I lost another young friend to AIDS and my younger brother, Robert, died at 51 from cancer. For a time, I talked to Robert nearly every Saturday morning. Once he said, "I guess God is trying to teach me something." To that I replied, "Well, I have never gone through anything that I did not learn something. I am sure you will too, but God may also want to teach someone else something."

Then a thought came to me which I believe must have come from the heart of God. I said, "I think the greatest compliment God can give one of His kids, is to let them go through a trial, because He knows He can trust them to walk through the experience in such a way as to bring glory to God." Robert did this with his cancer.

That November I was still living on the farm I mentioned earlier. I became very ill. I felt as though I had the flu, but it didn't get any better, no matter how much medicine I took. My illness carried over into the spring of 1992. I had no energy and could barely get out of bed.

At someone's suggestion, I finally went to the Oklahoma Allergy Clinic in Oklahoma City. The tests revealed that I was allergic to my total environment. Friends helped me try to sanitize the home I was living in, but it was old and I am sure there was lots of mold in the walls. I was getting sicker and sicker.

Some of my friends thought I was going to die on that farm. I think one more month there and they would have been right. I know this sounds very melodramatic, but it was, just that.

Finally, on Memorial Day 1992, I moved back to Dallas. My husband, Jack, stayed on the farm. I had been sick long enough that I had gone through my savings and returned to Dallas with $20 and one granola bar. I was so sick that it was difficult to work. I sold a little jewelry and a few cosmetics, both through direct sales companies in order to survive. My friends bought whatever I sold and occasionally would give me a little extra money. I was too sick to be proud.

In fact, I lived in a government subsidized apartment. It was very nice and had a big window in the living room which looked out onto a beautiful courtyard. It was a nice place to recover. The process was very slow. It was a hot summer and I had to wear a mask any time I went outside. In fact, I wore one a lot until 1996.

On the upside of this experience, I lived in a large apartment complex. No one there tried to play the "one-upmanship" game. We all knew that if we had any money we couldn't live there. The playing field was level. God was so good to me through my friends. I often say, "I was just a hair away from being in a box under a bridge."

I was in my early 50ies and you don't expect to lose your health at that age. I laugh and say that, "Yes, I might still live in a box someday, but if so, it will be the cutest box under that bridge. I will decorate it with lace and crayons that I find on the street." I don't know if you can understand, but there is something quite freeing about not fearing being old and without. I believe God will keep me healthy enough to work, or make me happy with what He gives me.

My relationship with Duane during this time was up and down. I didn't know it, but he was fighting his own demons. He was drinking and doing cocaine a lot by then. There may have been other drugs also, but he only told me this much.

During the last year of his life, Duane told me that he knew there were times I didn't have money for food and because of the drugs, he didn't even care that I was without. He said, "Mother, I was spending five thousand dollars a month on drugs and didn't care about you. That is what drugs will do to you. I am sorry now, Mother." Of course, I had forgiven him before he asked for it. Oh, how I loved that boy!

In the fall of 1992, Duane was fired from his purchasing job with Foley's. He had been drugged up and made a bad purchase. His boss hated to fire him because he was so well liked and had done a great job for them up until this time.

He checked himself into a hospital to dry out. If you know anything about drugs; one short stay is not long enough to get over them, but it did show him that he had a bigger problem than he realized.

Duane said, "I knew I was a drug addict, but at this time I realized I was also an alcoholic." I am sure I don't know all the facts, but he said he had to go to AA meetings. I don't know if it was a court order, but he did go.

If you have ever known anyone who has battled an addiction, you know it is a difficult matter. As Duane sobered up and looked at his life, he had to blame someone (at least at first) for the mistakes he had made. Because I was the one who had always been there for him, I was "it." These were difficult days for us. We were both physically ill and emotionally hurt.

The last time I went to the farm and spent a night, I thought I was surely going to die. On the way back to Dallas, I was so sick that I was weaving a little as I drove. About 30 miles north of Dallas, a cop stopped me. He asked if I had been drinking. When I told him no, he said he didn't think so, but that he was concerned about my driving. I said that I didn't feel good and that I would be careful. He didn't give me a ticket. He just asked me to stop and call 911 if I thought I couldn't make it home. I promised I would do that.

When I got to my apartment and got into the bed, I had a horrible experience. I felt like my eyes were floating like egg yolks. My head was spinning. I was so very sick at my stomach. I thought, "This must be what it feels like to be a drug addict and need a fix!" I knew if someone stepped to my side and said, "Take this and you will feel better, I probably would have." All this was from allergies to that farm. Allergies aren't just about runny noses and sneezes. They can kill you.

During this time of recovery, one of my friends was as steady as a rock. Sue Lacy will always be my hero. She kept me from starving during that year. She would call and ask, "What do you want to eat? We have coupons for Chinese or Mexican."

That Christmas, she and her daughter, Keri, who was in high school, decorated a small Christmas tree and brought it over in the back of a pick-up. Keri rode with the tree to keep it from turning over. I love remembering how good God has been to me and how He has provided for me over and over again, sometimes directly, usually through others.

Duane came to see me a couple of times that year. We were trying to be good to each other during this time while I was living with so many health challenges.

August was a very sad time for me. My nephew, Phil, had a heart attack and died immediately. I was crushed. He and I had developed a strong bond of love over the years. I was only twelve years older than he. His mother died in 1982, so he and I became even closer. We never had a harsh word between us.

I remember Phil once picked me up at the Tulsa airport and drove me up to Dewey to see my mother.

"I wish I had the kind of faith you and Grandma have," Phil said. I replied, "Well, you believe in Jesus Christ. Just read your Bible and pray and your faith will grow."

I do believe heartaches will either drive you closer to God or you will turn away and often become bitter. I am thankful that with every trial, I have grown closer to God. Often, I have climbed up on Father God's lap and said, "Abba, Father, hold me and let me feel your strength." Abba in Aramaic means Daddy. Jesus referred to Father God as Abba Father.

As I tell the offenders in prison, I think when my daddy died I poured out all my love for my daddy on God. I truly saw God as my Father. I am well aware that if you did not have a good earthly Father, it might be difficult for you to think of God as a good, kind, loving Father. I hope this book will give you just a little more openness to the thought of how much God loves you and wants a relationship with you.

I had talked to Phil about Duane and asked him to be there for Duane if something should happen to me. He had assured me that he would definitely stand by him. It never occurred to either of us that he would die first.

The fear of my dying before Duane was always at the back of my mind. I prayed many a night that God would spare me. I am so grateful that God granted me that request.

CHAPTER 4
AIDS Strikes

***

Near the end of January 1993, Duane called. "Mother, this is the Big One!" he exclaimed. "My doctor couldn't get me over my pneumonia, so she convinced me to have an HIV test. I have just learned that I have full-blown AIDS."

To be honest, I don't remember much of the rest of the conversation. I just know my entire world changed in that moment. I was hot, I was cold, and I thought I would die on the spot!

I remembered a day after Duane's father had left. He called me from Houston where he was working, and I had cried and begged him to come home and tell me what was wrong with me so I could fix it. After about 30 minutes of that, he said goodbye. I had looked for something to take that day to end it all. I had thought, "I can never hurt this badly again."

Here I was again, with my heart exploding inside my body. People wonder why I love my Lord so. I would have surely gone crazy without Him! My baby, my baby, my flesh, bone of my bone, blood of my blood–after all of these years of trying to keep my baby safe and healthy, how could this have happened? How could I deal with this? How could I help him deal with it? I was just so grateful that he loved and trusted me enough to be honest with me and tell me as soon as he knew.

Duane and I had talked about his behavior and the possibility that he was HIV positive and could die from AIDS but he had refused to be tested. There are some things for which you simply cannot prepare.

Even after all these years, I sob as I write. So why do I write? I write to tell you of the unconditional love, the eternal love of a mother for her son and his love for her. I write because Duane gave me that mandate to write and speak.

There was more bad news coming. My husband called from the farm on February 14th to wish me a happy anniversary, then five minutes later asked for a divorce.

I knew our marriage was probably not going to survive my moving back to Dallas. I couldn't survive physically on the farm and Jack didn't think he could make a living in Dallas, and the marriage was a struggle. The last thing I wanted on my record was another divorce! All I had ever wanted was to be a good wife and mother.

Life can surely throw us some curves, can't it? There were some fantastic times still ahead for me, but at this moment it felt like the end of my world. I can't tell you how much I appreciated my friends. Don't ever take your friends for granted. They are God's angels on earth.

The next couple of months were just awful! I cried and cried, but couldn't cry when speaking with Duane because he was being so brave. Man, what an attitude. I was so proud of him. He was determined to go on living as long as he possibly could. He said, "Mother, I am not dying from a fatal disease. I am living with a life threatening disease."

I made a lot of notes when I talked to Duane. I recently found one where he called me on February 18th. He said, "I'm scared–I feel hopeless–I have no job and am too sick to look for one." He had told his doctor it was okay to talk to me about his condition.

The doctor's nurse said, "Oh, we are so glad to hear from a family member. Most families don't want to deal with this at all."

The doctor and I developed a wonderful relationship over the years. She was rather young when she started caring for Duane, but the two of them along with my love and God's blessings kept him alive for almost six years.

The man that Duane lived with when he was diagnosed is still living because of early detection. I want to encourage all of you to be tested if you think you have ever done anything which could have exposed you to this virus. With proper medication and early detection, people are living for many years.

If you are doing anything which could expose you to this virus, stop–please stop. By the way, many people don't know that you can contract the AIDS virus through oral sex. I knew one boy who died from AIDS and that is how he was exposed. This is an awful disease to experience. If you know someone who has this disease, please pray for them and be kind to them. We don't have to affirm each other's behavior, but we certainly can love and respect each other.

As Jesus said, "He, who is without sin, cast the first stone." Then He turned to the accused and said, "Go and sin no more."

On February 22nd, we talked again; this time about how many people Duane knew who cared deeply about him. He had a lot of fears. He feared what would happen to him when his insurance would run out. He didn't want to look like he had AIDS. He was afraid of strangers looking at him.

Then he said, "That is all shallow stuff, I need to pray and be really confident that God will get me through it." And God did. He went on to say that what he needed was love and emotional support. He ended by saying, "I can't be spiritual if I'm having casual sex."

I don't remember just what happened between the 22nd and 28th, but evidently we had cross words. As my neighbor, Linda, says, "there were four T's…Trials, Tears, Torment, and Triumph."

I wrote the following note to myself and felt perhaps I should include it here. It shows the deep pain I was feeling at the time.

> *I am tired! Very, very tired! Death seems like an old friend that I would like to wrap up in and lie down and go to sleep in death. No, I am not suicidal, just weary, weary, weary. Yes, I know the Bible tells us not to be weary in well doing…it isn't the well doing I am tired of…it is all the failures (or what others see as failures) of my life that I am so sick and tired of (yes I know that isn't good sentence structure…I don't give a hoot)…Oh God I am so tired…if only my finances weren't so awful and my house such a mess I would like to come home to you Father…tonight…yes, I am having death wishes…I know that it is the chicken way out…I don't want to hurt any more…I am so tired of the pain of life…I want to be free of all of this…I can't get parenting right…I want it to be finished…over…through…done with…I can't be a good mother, wife, and that is all I ever really wanted to be…I feel like such a failure…now I have failed at business…I pray Father, for the rapture…I don't want to leave my mother; I used to say I didn't want to leave Duane…maybe he would be better off without me…that is so hard to accept…I have loved him so much…right now, I would like to scream…if I was in the country I would do just that…SCREAM!!!!*
>
> *One thing is for sure…I must find a support group…I am not going to make it on my own…seems like I should be able to handle this, just "me and Jesus"…it's not Duane's*

dying that is the problem...it is this interim period. Tonight Uncle Dud said to me "I have never known anyone with PCP [Pneumocystis Carinii Pneumonia] that was long term." I had just awakened when Duane called me. He started telling me that right now I was not what he needed, etc., and I made the mistake of telling him what Dud said. He got very upset with me...he does not want to think of not getting well. He is fighting to live...I want to think that way too, but I didn't want to stick my head in the sand and waste my time not seeing him. I just have to leave him alone and accept the fact that I am not what he wants in his life right now!

Duane made some remark about how his needs were the ones that need to be met. That is right...BUT...I have needs too and it is RIGHT for them to be met. No more am I going to be the typical Al-Anon and assume that everyone else is more important than me...so he has AIDS...I have a broken heart...and that is just as deadly and just as important...I am of value...not because I am so wonderful, but because GOD created me...it is okay for my feelings and wants and desires to be important... where Duane is concerned...where Jack is concerned... where Jim was concerned...OKAY so I wanted to cave in...I have confessed that to myself and to God...so I would welcome death...I WOULD...but until I die... and meet God in the air...I am going to fight...fight for my life, my feelings, my existence, my job, my future...I would like to die, but apparently God has not chosen to take me yet, so if I really trust Him, I have to believe that He knows what He is doing...if I love Him, I will put on my best face, my best smile, and get back into the race of life...I will put all this behind me, and think of what will be right for me...I DO LOVE YOU GOD...

AND YOU ARE ENOUGH...YOU AND I CAN AND WILL MAKE IT...OH, I WILL PROBABLY GOOF SOME MORE WITH DUANE, BUT SO BE IT...I AM NOT THE PERFECT MOTHER. BUT THEN...HE IS NOT THE PERFECT SON... HE HAS HURT ME A LOT SINCE NOVEMBER, WHEN HE SOBERED UP!! HIS HONESTY MAY BE HEALING HIM BUT IT SURE HAS HURT ME...I DON'T WANT TO FORGET WHAT HONESTY FEELS LIKE...PAIN...MAYBE WE NEED TO BE CAREFUL ABOUT HONESTY...

I am sure it is painful to read all this, but I pray it helps others to know their pain has been felt by someone else. One of the things life has taught me is that we don't have to have one-upmanship on pain. We all have our own pain and it hurts. Your pain is as important as anyone else's pain. Let's love each other and be patient with each other.

On March 10th Duane called and left a message stating he wanted to make amends. He said he had been upset, fearful and mad. So, once again, all was forgiven.

A couple of days later he yelled into the phone at me saying, "You did a horrible job raising me!" Remember, he had to blame someone for his choices and the consequences he was experiencing.

Perhaps it was because I was still sick, but I was very calm and also firm. I simply stated, "I can no longer participate in this conversation." I didn't slam it; I just quietly placed the phone on its cradle. I thought about it for a day or two, and then wrote Duane the following letter of resignation. I had not wanted it to be out of anger, hurt, or just a knee-jerk reaction.

Saturday, March 13, 1993
Dallas, Texas

My Darling Son,

This is without a doubt the most important letter of my life. I want you to know that I have loved being your mother. No matter where I go, people always ask me (immediately after saying hello), "How is Duane?" or "Where is Duane?" Everyone knows you because I have always had such glowing things to say about you. They were all true too. I've always said, "No matter what differences Duane and I have in the way we see life, he has been the most wonderful son any woman ever had." My love for you was surpassed only by my love for Jesus. You have been the most important person in my life.

So many of the decisions I have made these last few years were based on trying to prepare for this time in your life. I kept praying that you would change your behavior and be spared AIDS. I remember when I told Phil about you. I said, "In case something happens to me, I want someone from my family to be there for Duane." When I was having trouble making my house payments on Collins, I put the house up for sale. Then I heard about them running AIDS patients out of apartments. For a long time those poor ill people were not treated very well. I thought, "I can't sell this house. I have to have a place where I can bring Duane if he should become ill." That may seem like dumb thinking now, but for that time, it really wasn't. The times are totally different now. You have your daddy's support now (and I am so grateful), but you didn't then. I kept trying to make my marriage to Jack work for a number of reasons. One of them was to have a place for you.

All those years, I feared losing you to AIDS... instead, I have lost you to your sobriety. It would almost be funny, if it were not so sad!

When you were a little boy, I remember you being so upset because your teacher made the class lay your heads down because someone was bad. I told you that life wasn't fair. That was hard for you to understand. Since I had tried to be fair with you, you expected everyone else to be fair also. Well, life isn't fair. We have no choice about so many things in life. One of the first things is that we have no choice about who our parents are. We don't even choose to be born. Well, tonight, I am giving you your freedom. I am resigning as your Mother. I will not refer to you as my son. You belong to you...100%. I give up all rights as a parent. I feel so sorry for you, Duane. It must be an awful feeling to believe that your mother did a horrible job raising you. I love my mother so, and respect her so, and admire her so. There was a time when I was very important to you. I am truly sorry that you have lost what you once felt for me.

When your father left, it was like he plunged a dagger through my heart. It was a quick, clean death. I once told Jack it was as though he ran a knife up and down my arms so they bled all the time, but I couldn't die. Since November, you have kept me bleeding much of the time. Today, you plunged the knife completely through my heart. THANK YOU! It is easier to die than to just bleed all the time.

I know this all sounds crazy. I would not have believed it had I not lived it. You see, when you yelled, "You did a horrible job raising me," it sent an excruciating pain *through me...it was the dagger. I couldn't cry, because I was on my way for an interview. I was devastated. Then I realized that was the end. We had nothing else to say to each other. For you see, I KNOW, I have been a wonderful mother and no, I wasn't perfect, and no, you weren't perfect, but you were not only a wonderful son, but a wonderful person. Yes, we need to always work on those things in our being which are undesirable, but no; we don't have to throw out the baby with the bath water. Your statement was a lie. If you believe it to be true, then you need to be released from our relationship. For every bad memory you have of me, I have 10 good ones of us. For every bad thing I ever did where you were concerned there were 10 or more good things I did...I was there TOO.*

Yes, you have a right to demand your money. I have had my rights over the years, which I chose not to demand, because you were my son. I knew you had criticized me for many things. Until today, I didn't understand the depth of your criticism. No wonder you want your money. You don't like me at all, do you? That is your choice. I really do understand the Serenity Prayer. I know I can't change the way you feel about me or what you believe to be true about me. I am so very grateful that I know who I am and what I am. I do have things I am working on...and I always will...every time I clean up one thing, God holds up the mirror to my heart and says, "Oh Elaine, look over here at this dirty spot." We (He and I) better start working on this one." One of my good qualities is that I am persistent. The downside of that is that sometimes I hang on too long. Today, I knew it was over. There wasn't anything I could say or do...It is finished.

Don't misquote me. I am not disowning you. I am resigning as your mother. I will always love you...I will always love all the wonderful times we have had together...I am grateful for all I did to try to understand you (going to a gay bar, a gay church, listening for hours about details, accepting your friends, being more than nice to them, reading, praying, listening to programs on TV, even having those two boys stay with us—don't know if that was wise—but I can't be accused of not giving it the "old college try")...I have regrets over the unwise decisions I made, but I have no guilt...none at all...I have asked God for forgiveness, I have asked for your forgiveness many times for things I did...I have accepted God's forgiveness...and furthermore, I have forgiven myself. For your sake I hope that you, too, can forgive me.

Sometime, later, down the line, if you want to discuss your adopting me as your mother, I will be open to the discussion. It will be a matter of you choosing me for a mother; not being born to someone you see as such a failure as a mother. I wish you happiness, a great sobriety, and I will respect your right to your own life.

Elaine

Duane and I did not discuss the letter. However, in a week or so he called and talked like nothing had happened. I assumed he still wanted me for his mother.

One day during the last couple of weeks of his life, as we sat on his bed talking, he began to giggle. When I asked what was so funny, Duane replied, "Do you know what one of the smartest things you ever did was?"

When I confessed that I didn't know, he laughed and said, "You resigned as my mother!" We both had a hearty laugh and hugged each other. Then he said, "It really made me think what it would be like if I didn't have you. I didn't like the way I felt."

Life isn't easy and sometimes it takes lots of effort to make relationships work. Some of our decisions are right and some are wrong. I have never been really good about setting boundaries. I think that is what that letter did. It said that he couldn't say just anything he wanted to say to me, but he could tell me how he felt if he did it in a nice way. That is the way we had communicated most of his life. He just had to blame someone for the mistakes he had made; just think how difficult all this was for him. It must be very scary to be so angry with the one person who has loved you and cared for you during your entire life.

Duane and I always got past our difficulties, because of our undying love for each other. As it turned out, our really tough times were not over.

One Sunday a few months after his diagnosis, he called and left a beautiful message on my answering machine. "Mother, I have had a glorious day. I went to a great AA meeting and met some wonderful people. Since it was a beautiful day in Houston, I took the top off my Samurai, and went riding around. You know, sometimes shit just happens. You make the best of it and thank God for every good moment you have. I just wanted you to know that I am okay."

Here's a little insight into my mind. You may remember, my daddy died when I was 12. I remember lots of the things he said to me, but I cannot remember how his voice sounded. I knew I would miss the sound of Duane's voice when he was gone.

Over the years, I kept many answering machine tapes. From them, I made a 30 minute tape of Duane's messages to me. The previous words were directly from that tape. When I really need to hear his voice, I play the tape. It is a wonderful comfort to me.

Once Duane was diagnosed with AIDS, my concern was totally focused on his eternal life. I asked all my prayer partners to pray that he would return to his faith in Jesus Christ. It was a long road, but it did happen.

I have shared much of Duane's story during various speaking engagements. Writing this all down for the whole world to read is more challenging. You can't see my facial expressions or hear the inflections in my voice. Remember, this is about a mother's unconditional love for her son! He and I win!

If you are getting disoriented reading this, just think what it was like to live it. At times Duane was loving and reaching out to me, but then he would strike out and bite me like a snake. I am sure I was not always rational either.

Not all was bad during 1993. The company that had let me go called me back to work. God does answer prayers. When things get bad enough, our false pride flies out the window. When I got the call, my boss said he couldn't pay me as well as he had before. I ended up going back for half of my former salary. Instead of a larger, nicer car, I got an economical blue Ford Tempo. It got me where I needed to go. I had enough for a modest apartment and I had health care. I loved the company and was grateful to be working again.

Duane knew I might be moving to Kansas City so he drove up from Houston to visit me. For the most part we had a lovely visit and shared a lot of laughter. At one point, he stood trembling all over and begged me to tell him that his lifestyle was okay. I wanted to do so, but I knew I couldn't. It was so hard for me not to tell him what he wanted to hear. I loved him so! We would have both known it was a lie.

Then he looked at me and said with tears running down his face, "Mother, I have not forgotten everything I learned at First Baptist. Every time we sang *Jesus Is Calling*, I just wanted to run to Him and tell Him I loved Him and beg for

His forgiveness." We embraced and cried and expressed our love for each other.

The night before I left for Kansas City I was praying over Duane that God would help him with all his struggles. I must have stirred things up because the next morning something very unusual happened.

We were having a good time, laughing and talking. I was packing my bag to fly to Kansas City for a final interview. Duane was sitting on the couch and had been encouraging me. All at once he spoke in a very deep, gravelly voice which was not his own.

He said, "That is the awfullest thing you can tell a little boy! That he is so bad that God had to come down out of the sky and hang on a cross because of him! In a way, you are my creator. You created me in your tummy."

I had never encountered such a spirit, but I stayed totally calm. "Duane," I said, "I taught you the truth as I believed it to be and still believe it to be. You are a grown man and can do with it what you will." Inside, I thought, "If you see me as your creator, you don't have to deal with your real creator, who is God."

I know this sounds off the wall, but remember that my beautiful son was struggling so with his addictions and his faith questions. Instinctively, I knew I was dealing with an evil power and I stayed calm and loving.

I told Duane that I loved him with all my heart as I left for the airport. As always, he told me he loved me too. He had a key to my apartment and intended to leave after I left.

I was in KC for a couple of days. I met with the officers of the company and we came to an agreement. I searched for an apartment, and found a nice place with a great view of the sunrises from my bedroom and the sunsets from my living room.

It was a lovely little apartment in Gladstone, Missouri just north of Kansas City. I chose to live there as it was near the airport. I wanted to be close in case I had to get to the airport in the snow for a business trip.

When I returned to Dallas from the interview, Duane had not left, and we had a sweet time before I moved. We never talked about the evil words which had come from his mouth. In fact, I am not sure he was even aware of the encounter. I knew there was a fight going on between good and evil. God won!

Drugs do such horrible things to people. The last year of Duane's life, we talked off and on about the time in his life when he was doing drugs.

Duane told me sometimes he dug around in the carpet looking for a grain of cocaine. He said that you get THAT desperate for your next fix.

For those of us that have never suffered from that kind of addiction, it is hard to understand what a terrible hold drugs can have on a person. The really sad thing is that no one sets out to be addicted. Everyone thinks they can quit whatever it is, alcohol or drugs or pornography or anything, right up until the time they can't quit. Then it is too late. They are addicted and it is a long, hard road back to sobriety.

I am proud and thankful that with counseling and the help of AA, Duane did give up alcohol and drugs. However, he had done great damage to his body, in fact to his life.

These two or three years were our most difficult ones. During the last year he lived he said, "Mother, after I am gone, if you find something that I wrote about you when I was coming off alcohol and drugs, please don't read it. You and I are in such a wonderful place now, but I was so angry at you then. I had to blame someone for the mess I had made of my life and you were the only one who was always there for me, so I blamed you."

Moving is never easy. Mine was no different. With things at both the farm and my apartment, it was complicated and I was still not totally well. My step-daughter, Sandee from Ardmore came, took me by the farm, and then drove me to the airport in Oklahoma City to catch a plane to Kansas City. My furniture did not catch up with me for several days.

I took with me a few things to wear to work, my cosmetics, a sheet, and a small pillow for my head. Of course, by the time I got to my new apartment, I was exhausted. I remember lying on the floor with the sheet under me and wrapped over me. It was the end of June, so it was hot, however, with air conditioning, I was comfortable.

I thought, "This must be how a homeless person feels in a shelter." I was cool and I was safe and I had a job, so I had a future. Little is much when seen through the eyes of appreciation!

I didn't have a company car yet, so one of the girls who lived near me gave me a ride to work. In fact, that same woman did the first editing of this book. She and I worked together at Luzier Cosmetics on many writing projects. She always said she would edit my book one day, but I know she had probably begun to believe this book would never be written. God wouldn't let me off the hook. He said, "Write the book."

I loved being back at a job that I enjoyed so much. I supervised our sales force of fabulous women. It was fun, challenging, and rewarding. It felt good to be productive again.

When the girls in the office heard that I was sleeping on the floor until my furniture arrived, they gathered things for my comfort. One loaned me a cot, someone else a blanket, and yet another, a real pillow. There are a lot of very neat people in the world. Thanks ladies!

I can still remember how it felt when I made my first trip to hold a business meeting. I got on the airplane, buckled my seat belt and thought, "I'm back! This is really me." I'm grateful for all the Craven family who own the company for the opportunity they gave me to grow, not only in business, but personally.

My CEO, Keith Craven, had a phrase he spoke to me a couple of times and I have never forgotten it. Keith said, "Don't tell me you will try to do it. Tell me you are going to do it!" That is a good way to live.

God had solved my financial struggles, but He was still working on my relationship with my son. I knew Duane did not want me to speak to him of Christ, but every now and then, I goofed by saying something.

One Saturday I heard this wonderful tape by an inspirational speaker. I was so moved and did the worst thing I could have done. I called and left a message for Duane about how blessed I had been by hearing this man speak. Wow! Wrong thing to do!

Duane called back and left this message, "Don't ever call me again!"

After crying and praying and asking God to forgive me for being unwise, I called the husband of one of my best friends back on the farm. My wise friend, Marvin, said, "Don't stop calling him, but don't call too often and just say, "Hi Honey. I just called to say hello and tell you I love you." That was good advice.

On December 16th, 1993, I was sitting in my office, deep into my work, when the phone rang. It was Duane. We talked for maybe an hour. All was well with us again. He had gotten the Christmas box I had sent. He had told me in November that he was going to stay in Houston for Christmas. This was our first time to be apart at this time of the year. We had always enjoyed this holiday so much. Expressing our love through gift giving was such fun for us. We always loved what the other gave, whether a small gift or like my beautiful leather coat, a lavish gift.

Duane said that his new apartment was the most beautiful home he had ever had since leaving our home. He wished I could see it. He said, "I consider it a gift from God."

He talked about the fact that he was intellectually mature but very immature emotionally. He went on to say that AIDS had been a gift to him. It forced him to make peace with God and with himself.

At an AIDS workshop he wrote a love letter to himself and another one to him from God. He went on to say, "I used to think that was a bunch of bull when you said, God gave me that thought; now I understand." Following is the letter he wrote from God as he struggled to overcome his addictions:

You are my child, and I love you. You were born with infinite love and compassion in your heart; love to give and to have returned. Wherever you go, whatever you do, I will love you always, unconditionally with all the power of the infinite universe. My love for you makes me suffer pain when you are sad. My love for you makes me rejoice when you are glad. Although I can't protect you from pain, evil, hurt, and accident, I will always give you the strength of my Spirit to see you through whatever may come. I will hear you when you cry, when you laugh, and even when you turn your back on me. No power in the universe can keep my love from you. You are my most precious child, forever and always, without fail.

Even after writing this letter, he went on a binge, and then did his AA 4th and 5th steps. He asked himself, "What is my part in this?" Then he told me it was not my responsibility. When he said, "It has been wonderful...really wonderful talking to you," my heart nearly burst with love. There was so much love in his voice, not just his words! It was like winning the greatest prize in the world. I have written this from long notes I took that day as we spoke. At the bottom of the last page I wrote, "My Best Christmas Gift Ever!"

Immediately upon saying goodbye to Duane, I jumped up, ran down two doors to my friend Linda's office and all but screamed, "My son has come home! Kill the fatted calf, bring a robe and ring!" (For the "Prodigal son" story in the Bible, see Luke 15:11–32.)

Linda and I hugged, cried, and prayed a prayer of thanksgiving to God for returning my son to me.

After I collected myself a little, I shared my story with Keith and offered to pay for the lengthy call. He said not to worry about it. He went on to say how he admired the way I was handling Duane's illness.

Keith added, "We are just not supposed to bury our children. There is nothing like a mother's love. Even in the wild, a mama animal will fight the biggest animal in the jungle to protect her young." He really did get it. Keith was and is very much a family man and I so appreciated his kindness to me.

Have you ever noticed how often God shows up at unexpected times and in unexpected ways? Again, one day I was working at my desk, not thinking about God or Duane or anything other than my job.

All at once, I felt a feeling of strength starting at my feet and rising like an elevator all the way to and through the top of my head. All I could think was it felt like incense rising through my body. To myself I said, "Oh, God, I knew You would give me strength, I just didn't know when!" That was it. This time God didn't say anything. He just did something in me and to me and for me. This was His strength given to me to deal with Duane's illness. In future times, when I had something very difficult to deal with, I just closed my eyes and felt God's strength rising up in me once again.

You see, as many of you know, once you have a real experience with God, nothing can take that away from you, not time, nor people, nothing! The apostle Paul wrote it a little differently in the Bible. To paraphrase, Romans 8:38–39 says, "Nothing can separate us from the love of God that is in Christ Jesus, our Lord; not height, nor depth, nor anything else in all creation."

Even as God was drawing Duane closer, his body was showing signs of the progression of his illness. On January 3, 1994 he was having a very bad day. I guess he was doing telephone sales then, because he said he had over one thousand dollars in sales. Something had gone wrong during a call and he hung up on a man, which was totally out of character for him. Duane ended up soiling his pants and going home.

Humiliated, he said, "I may have to wear Depends." He went on to say that right before Christmas, he was cramping so badly one day he thought he was going to die. The really neat thing was that he went on to say, "Last week was fabulous." He was so courageous.

Duane was on a lot of medication, which was an expense that was hard for him. However, he said, "When I need money, God puts money in my hands." From time to time, I helped him get prescriptions. Sometime during the last year, he confessed that he had spent the $2.50 gold piece I had given him on drugs.

Quickly, he said, "Mother, prescription drugs. I would never have bought illegal drugs with that. It was so special, because you gave it to me." I don't think I told him, but I had wondered if it was spent for the wrong kind of drugs. It was nice to know that it was for medication which he needed so badly.

In January 1994, Duane's dad was talking about coming from Dallas to see him. He had called one day when Duane was really, really sick and seemed shaken by Duane's response. In fact, Jim called Duane three times in two weeks, which was unusual.

Duane recalled an exercise in an AA meeting where everyone had to picture their parents growing up to understand why they are the way they are now.

"I could see you, but not Daddy," Duane commented. "I know so little about him."

Then he said, "I really expect you to love me unconditionally, but I haven't always been that way with you. I expect too much of you. I expect you to be perfect."

My response was simple. I said, "I really do love you like the letter God wrote to you but I couldn't always express it in a way that you totally understood."

I felt sorry for Duane's daddy at Duane's memorial service in Houston. His friends got up and spoke so highly of Duane and I thought, "His daddy doesn't even know the man they are speaking of so highly. He never took the time as he was growing up to get to know him." Jim did reach out to Duane from time to time those last years.

Jim was not a bad person. After all, I had loved him with all my heart for 18 years. Even after our divorce, it was hard to get over him. Jim just could not seem to embrace his son. Even though Duane knew I loved him, he still needed his father's love.

I took copious notes during the remainder of Duane's life, so I am going to share some quotes from those notes to show you the flavor of his life. I have often said Duane raised the bar on how to live with a life threatening disease. Truly, I was amazed at how mature he really became.

1-19-94

"I changed my old number to this one so my friends can find me." I said, "What?" Then he laughed really big and said, "It's a joke, Mother!" Ha, ha! Yes, he knew there were some friends that were not good for him anymore. He had such a good sense of humor.

1-30-94

I wrote, "Just had a wonderful conversation with Duane. We talked about an hour. We covered a lot of heavy—very important issues. (I do love him so!)" To the side I wrote, "He is such a neat person." From the conversation I could tell that he was feeling better. For two weeks he hadn't had diarrhea, now it was back. Even though he had lost his job at Foley's, he was still working from time to time. At this time his job was not as physical, but more stressful. He had a friend who had just died and another who was in the hospital.

He went on to say, "I'm not going to commit suicide. Well, maybe I would. I'm not making plans."

Can you begin to imagine the pain we both experienced because of this disease? How can anyone think God is not a loving Father, just because He says we are not to have sex outside of marriage between a man and woman? Surely, God does not want any of us to suffer like this!

We then talked about cremation. He said he didn't care. He said that if there was any part of his body that could be used, he would want it to be done.

Duane said, "I have not trusted you." I asked, "In what area?" (You think I am not brave?) He replied, "I have nightmares thinking I will be hooked up to tubes and you will lay hands on me and pray to Jesus." I don't know how I responded to that, but he went on to say, "I love you very much. I know I've done a lot to hurt you. I apologize. I appreciate you so!"

He then told me that his hair was starting to thin. Every day his hair was coming out. He had always had beautiful, almost black hair. Right before we said "I love you" to each other, he said with a deep sadness in his voice, "I have lots of regrets."

As I read all this, I wonder how we kept going. It had to have been God's love for us and our love for each other. We simply were not going to let this life and disease defeat us. Keep remembering...we win in the end!

2–18–94

"I'm having a rough time mentally. I am crying a lot. My insurance runs out in May. I feel so alone." His daddy said, "Well, this is something you have to do alone. If I could do it for you, I would." That was a nice thing to say. However, the difference between Jim's take on things and mine was that I knew Duane didn't have to do it alone; I was walking with him and I was praying for him. So whether he knew it or not, God was helping him all the way.

Sometimes Duane would talk a few minutes then say, "I'm dealing with a lot and I don't want to talk about it." Those were the times we just said, "I love you" and hung up the phones.

I helped Duane financially from time to time, but he didn't ask for much. I paid for his phone calls to me. They were worth every penny I spent on them. Our calls were the lifeline between us.

5-2-94

Duane had lost 20 pounds from a parasite problem known as Cryptosporidium. About that time quite a number of people in Minnesota had died from the same parasite which had gotten in the water supply. It was a miracle Duane didn't die then. In fact, he carried that in his body until he died in 1998. It caused diarrhea and vomiting. The surprising thing was, the sicker he became, the more he desired to live!

5-16-94

"I have been to the dermatologist. I have sores (Molescums) on my face from a virus. I have a lot of anger at you. I still love you. Sometimes I feel compassion for what you went through, sometimes I am just mad at you."

I replied, "You may call me to vent. I will listen. I won't defend myself or make excuses."

He then said, "Bye Sweetie."

5-20-94

I talked to Duane's doctor. We spoke of the parasite and his weight loss. She was very concerned about him, and was doing the paper work for a study. She was a wonderful, caring, and loving doctor. I spoke with

Duane that same day. He was making himself a cake. He said, "No special reason. I'm just being good to Duane."

5-23-94

Duane's 31st birthday. We spoke about how good his friends had been to him over the months. Then he said his dad had come down and they had a good visit. He tensed up when I said, "You know I will come down if you ever want me, but I won't be pushy about it. I love and respect you." I went on to say, "I'm glad you have a better relationship with your father. I know you have always wanted that." We were having difficulty talking, so we both said, "I love you." He thanked me for calling and thanked me for the two place settings of my china I sent to him. Wish I could serve him a meal on it tonight!

5-28-94

Duane had lost 32 pounds. He was trying Marinol by this time, which is made from marijuana. He was also on D4T, which was an alternate to AZT, because he couldn't tolerate that drug. This night we talked a lot about his early years. He said that after school was a nightmare for him. He was chased home four out of five afternoons.

As we continued talking, he said that his father had recently been able to be expressive, loving, and supportive. Jim told him that he was glad Duane was his son. Duane replied, "I tried to prove something to you."

After talking for quite some time, Duane said, "I love you very much. It's hard to separate what's about *you and what's about me." Perhaps this will help you to see how hard it is for some people to go through the process of getting sober and staying sober.*

We have looked at a lot of Duane's struggles. Here is something I wrote on 5-31-94: *I really struggled today with the reality of Duane's death...talked to Keith (remember, he was my boss)...he so sweet...said when I need to go...go...don't worry about job, Ks. City...take care of priorities...Difficult evening...wanted to cry and scream at the same time...talked to my sis, Jean, from Ardmore...did help...she said when God has broken Duane it would be the sweetest time of our lives.* She turned out to be right, but there were still difficult days ahead for us.

6-1-94

I wrote: *Bad time trying to get up...know it is state of denial...Heard the song CELEBRATE...GOT MY FOCUS OFF MYSELF, BACK ONTO JESUS... HEARD PREACHER SAYING, "Why not me?" Yes, why not me? Why should I not have to suffer? There was a time in my past when this thought brought me back to a right thinking and feeling, "SO FORGET ABOUT MYSELF AND WORSHIP HIM!" THAT'S THE SECRET...LOOKING TO JESUS, NOT TO MY PROBLEM!! PRAISE THE LORD!!*

6-2-94

After having two very difficult days, I was happy to hear Duane's voice. He said, "I really want to talk to you. I thought a lot of you today. I am tired of being angry. Really like to start over. I'm just emotionally weary. I've had a pretty good day. Really tired. Went to a noon AA meeting, had lunch, and napped. Tomorrow afternoon there is a State AA Convention." He had tried a drug made from opium and it really scared him. He said he couldn't take any drug derived from an addictive substance as he had bad reactions to it.

* * *

Some time that spring, I drove from Kansas City to Dewey, Oklahoma where I grew up to see my mother and tell her that Duane had AIDS. That was one of the hardest things I ever did. Have I already told you about how my parents were always telling me to "be brave"?

It was dusk as I drove into the north side of town. I passed right by the cemetery. Now, I am not much of a cemetery person. I know my loved ones are not there, but in Heaven. However, the closer I got to the cemetery, the more I wanted and needed to talk to my Daddy. So, yes, I stopped. I said something like this, "Daddy, I need a big dose of that bravery you were always talking to me about. How am I going to tell Mother that my precious, baby boy has AIDS?"

I don't remember if I prayed, but knowing me, I probably did. This is so raw, I cry as I write. Without God, I would have never made it…From a human standpoint, Duane and I carried the awful burden of homosexuality and AIDS all alone but Father God, Jesus, and the Holy Spirit buoyed me up through it all.

When I got to my mother's, we were so happy to see each other. We talked and talked like we always did. I couldn't bring myself to tell her about Duane. The family was coming for lunch the next day. I had already told my two sisters. This first night with my mother was perfect.

The next morning, I went out back where my brother and sister-in-law lived. Since they were close by mother could continue living alone. My brother, John, was so sweet to me. He assured me it wasn't my fault. I knew his wife, Gay, would be sweet about my news, because she had always shown Duane lots of love when we had visited the family.

Who knows, maybe the way I raised Duane contributed to his choices, but if so I had asked God's forgiveness many years before. As one gay man said to him when he was in high school, "I can see your mother taught you how to love. You are just expressing it in an improper way." Interesting coming from a gay man, don't you think?

After speaking with John, I went into the house to put on my makeup before everyone arrived. Like she usually did, mother came into the bathroom to talk while I got ready. She was sitting right there looking up at me.

I said, "Mother, when I told you the other night that Duane is really sick, did you understand that it is serious?" She said, "Yes, Honey, I did."

Looking straight into her sweet eyes, I said, "Mother, he has an incurable disease." Without blinking an eye, she asked, "Is it AIDS?" I said, "Yes, Mother, it is."

I remember all of that as though it were yesterday. However, I can't tell you one more thing about that trip. I guess I was in such a state of shock. I had dealt with Duane's disease for over a year, but somehow, telling my mother made it real and almost unbearable for me.

CHAPTER 5

Life Goes On

* * *

On June 23rd, Duane said he was taking Marinol twice a day. I told him I admired him for fighting this disease. He said he had a nice talk with Grandma Webber (my mother). She had been very supportive of him. I said, "I know the family didn't always show they loved you, but they do." He had been to a support group discussing the value of receiving. He was feeling very grateful.

Five days later, on the 28th we talked again. He had been really sick that day. He had slept most of the weekend. Saturday night he had been to a party. He had an uncomfortable experience as he sat on the couch. All at once, he was stoned from his medication. Now, today, he was losing his train of thought.

On July 1st, as we talked, I asked him if he would like to go to Oklahoma to see my family. We talked about the time they didn't want me to come home after my friend died. After facing the fact, they might reject us, he said, "I would like to see my Grandma one more time." We decided to go on July 23rd. I don't remember how receptive they were, but my family did agree that we could come.

On July 11th Duane said, "I was with Dad and Liz over the weekend. We went to Galveston. I had a good time, although I overdid it a bit. I was a little short of breath." Again, I was happy for both he and his father. I told him I was sending tickets and money for his trip to Oklahoma. He told me he appreciated me trying to meet his needs. He was pleased that his Aunt Evelyn had called for the AA meeting times and location.

Duane was flying from Houston to Tulsa. I was picking him up and driving to the Bartlesville/Dewey area.

The family was wonderful. We stayed at a motel, but went to both Evelyn's and Mother's. While sitting on the bed at the motel, I asked him if he would like for me to rub his back. He had always loved that. Even through his shirt, I was shocked to feel how boney he was. Yes, he was extremely thin.

While we were there, I got sick with a stomach virus. Evelyn ended up driving him to the AA meeting.

Once at Eve and Dave's, Duane and I were sitting on the couch. All at once, without warning, I started to cry. He put his arm around me and told me it was okay, that I had been really strong and he knew I was hurting.

After he got home on July 25th, he said, "I really enjoyed our visit. We worked hard and we deserve a pat on the back." He went on to say he tried not to be sensitive, especially with me. He felt the trip was successful. He said, "I am on borrowed time. I owe time to God."

Aside from my work and Duane, I kept myself busy. I became a member of the Gladstone Chamber of Commerce, and sat on the board for two years.

I joined a small Southern Baptist church near my apartment, and worked in its missions to the homeless and aging.

I even managed to date briefly again. A man I met in my apartment complex asked me to dinner, and we continued dating for about six months until he said, "I think you need to date someone who can go to church with you and enjoy your spiritual side." I appreciated his honesty.

As it turned out, I never dated anyone else while in Kansas City. Little did I know what God had in mind for me. When I returned to Dallas and had dinner with my old friend, Dudley, there was no man in my head or heart. No one had to move out of my emotions, so that he could move into my heart.

You can see that with my job, the Chamber, and my church, I had a very fulfilling life. The only blot on my life was the times Duane was unhappy with me but things were getting better for us.

I never want this book to sound like a "pity party for me." However, I do hope people will cut parents a little slack if they are upset about their children's behavior. Any destructive behavior hurts parents, as well as the children, other relatives, and friends. There is no such thing as isolated sin. Sometimes it is our lifestyle, sometimes our actions, sometimes our attitude that cuts people into little pieces. My prayer is that our story will bring healing, understanding, and even acceptance of each other, even if we cannot always affirm each other's behavior.

In August, Duane was fitted with a leg brace because of pain from a pinched nerve at the base of his spine. It helped some. He had such a tender heart. One day he said he had an experience that touched him deeply. He saw a woman and a little girl going through the garbage. At first, he wanted to get indignant, but didn't. Instead, he said, "Here is another can." She smiled really big.

August was a "so-so" month for Duane physically. In many of my notes, he was feeling pretty good, but tired. Sometimes there was real pain. We often talked for only a few minutes. One notation went like this, "Don't feel up to talking. I appreciate your call. I love you."

One day when he wasn't feeling well, he said, "I think you sometimes crossed my physical boundaries. It is okay to touch my hands or arms, not my face or chest. I don't think I went through the phase of a little boy who says, 'don't touch me', I think I am there now."

To all of this I said, "I think when something happens you will want me." To which he replied, as he laughed, "Think I will too. Went for a blood transfusion one day and felt abandoned. Yes, I will want you."

You will see, the last two years of his life, every time he went to the hospital, one of the first questions they asked was, "Where is your mother." He would say, "She is on her way from Dallas."

The memorial service for his friend was the first part of September. I sent a lovely bouquet of flowers. Duane said, "Mother that was so sweet of you." He knew I was still on a close budget, so, yes, it was a sacrifice on my part. You see, even though I didn't want Duane in the lifestyle, I never dishonored him or his friends.

Duane has been gone 14 years and I just talked with the man he was in a relationship with at the end of his life. Yesterday, I sent by e-mail to his friend, what I had written about Duane's last day with me on earth, his first with Jesus. These are his words:

I am positive that your book will help to heal many wounds in people that cannot forgive or accept others;
I have no doubt that you have a superior mission to accomplish always guided by Jesus.
Love you so very much. Juan

You see, no matter what anyone thinks, I am not judgmental just because I stand on what the Bible says. My goodness, I have been married four times. Who am I to judge anyone?

Even though I know I have been forgiven, I don't want the church or anyone to tell us that our sins are not sins. That doesn't help us. To improve any behavior, we have to know it is wrong!

Did I tell you what my darling little granddaughter, Rachel, said about my marriages? She was about eight or nine years old. They had spent the night with me. Her sister, Sarah, was still sleeping and Rachel and I were on the couch. I don't know what prompted her, but she said, so matter-of-fact, "Well, Nonnie, you know you've been married three times." Inside, I thought, "Oh, no. I knew we would have this conversation sometime, but when she is this age?!"

Calmly, I said, "Honey, you know I have talked to you girls about not telling the truth. I am embarrassed to tell you, but I have actually been married four times." Quickly, with no sound of condemnation, she replied, "Well, Nonnie, you sure got it right the last time!" Of course, she was speaking of my marriage to her special grandfather, Dudley Dancer. I said, "Yes, I did." End of conversation. She has never mentioned it to her family or again to me. It is a settled issue with her and with God.

Often my prayers for Duane were simple. Such as, "God give him a day without pain." On August 28, 1994, my phone notations said we talked about his job at the Decorative Center, about our relationship, about my prayer–Duane to Heaven. I'm not sure what prayer I was referring to, but I guess he let me speak of it.

Sometime while in Kansas City, I began to pray: "Jesus I had to trust You for my salvation and I am trusting You for the salvation of my son, Duane. If at his point of death, he is still confused about what he believes about You, I am asking You to show up personally. Hold Your hand out and say, "Duane, I am Jesus. I am Who your Mother told you I am. Take My hand, and I will take you to the Father."

I have never heard anyone say anything like that. I truly believe God gave me that prayer through the power of The Holy Spirit. At the time, I didn't know if I would ever hear Duane declare his belief in Jesus as his Savior again. As God would have it, that did happen, and in a very unusual way, but we aren't there yet.

I have prayed that same prayer for others who are not believers. It is only through the power of The Holy Spirit that any of us come to Christ.

I have confessed that I used to think (still catch myself) that if I just spoke slowly enough and used clear enough words, I could make anyone believe what I believe. Not a chance! Ha, ha. Relax and enjoy the book. I am not going to change you. I am not trying. However, I have learned from other people all my life. Maybe there is something you can apply to your life. If so, use it, share it with others. Let's flood the world with real love, the kind that is honest, but always gentle.

It was about this time, that I shared with some of my oldest friends about Duane's illness. We needed all the support and prayers we could get. My sister, Evelyn, put him on the prayer chain at the Dewey Methodist church I attended as a child and teenager. I got cards from lots of friends saying they were praying for me and for Duane. It was such a comfort.

A portion of my journal entry for August 21, 1994: The meditation for today reads, "Lord, help me put aside the things that are breaking my heart, to pray for the things that are breaking Your heart. Amen."

Isn't that one of the most beautiful thoughts you have ever heard? I began to cry for my child, my baby, who is hurting so badly in so many ways...I thought how God's heart must be so broken at all the sadness in our world, of all the lost souls. I ask God to help me live a life of witness for Him.

My prayer is, "Father, as much as I love Duane, I know that I don't even begin to know how to love. Some will come to the gates of Heaven and say, 'I did this and that in Your name, and You will say, "I never knew you." Duane will say, "God, I do believe, help me in my unbelief." God will say, "Come here son; let me hold you and tell you more about my first Son, Jesus."

I couldn't stop crying. I got my Bible and just rubbed its cover and pulled it close to me and ask God to hold me. I praised our God until I could stop sobbing. Now as I write, the tears flow gently, soothingly down my face. How I love my Jesus! How grateful I am that my mother took me to church when I was two weeks old. My heavenly Father and Jesus are as real to me as my mother and father. It has only been the last 30 or 35 years that I have come to understand and appreciate and love the Holy Spirit.

Why do I share my sorrow and grief with you? It is so you will know that when these times of deep pain overcame me, I ran to the one person, my Friend, my Savior, my Husband, my beloved Jesus, who could really get me through the pain to the other side where the pain can be used for my spiritual growth and others' benefit. I am so thankful for God's mercy.

8–21–94

Again, from my notes–Duane called me at a hotel this morning where I was conducting a meeting. He got me just before I started my presentation. We had talked yesterday. He thought he might need to talk to me. He had a friend who left the hospital yesterday to go home to die. Duane saw him last night and needed to talk about it. After a time, as with any incurable disease, people are ready to quit fighting and just die to be relieved of their body.

Duane and I talked about his own death. I confessed that sometimes I just pretend he is going to be overseas where I wouldn't be able to see him for a long time. We know the phone service isn't that great everywhere, so I wouldn't be able to talk to him. One day, though, I could go and be with him again.

I also shared with him that last week as I was thinking about him, I told a couple of the girls at the office (this is a real growing experience for them too) that I could just hear my daddy (that Duane never knew), my sister, Ruth (Duane adored), and my brother, Robert saying, "You know, we feel sad for Elaine, but we can hardly wait for Duane to get up here to Heaven." They are getting a party together to celebrate his arrival. My loss will be their gain.

My relationship with Duane is taking on the sweetness it once had. He is reaching out to me again.

* * *

By September, he was seriously thinking of the end. I think they encouraged this at some of the support groups. On the 12th, he called to say he had written a will with me as the beneficiary and independent executor. He had named me as his Medical Power of Attorney, with his dad next, and in third place, his step-mother, Liz. I was also his Financial POA. We discussed what he wanted and didn't want at the end of his life. He didn't want extraordinary measures, but I will tell you, at your time of death, you need someone you can trust. For you see, when it comes right down to it, we usually want to hold on to life as long as possible. When Duane died, he was still on TPN, which is nutrition through a line.

This was also the time he signed his Doctors' Directive. If you have not taken care of these things, I urge you to do so. Signing all these papers won't make you die. It just makes it easier on your loved ones and you have your wishes fulfilled as much as possible.

Life Goes On

Over the years, his doctor and I conversed many times. I felt so close to her and she was so glad I took such an active part in Duane's life.

The funny or perhaps I should say interesting thing about life is that no matter what difficult things we are dealing with, life still goes on. Sometimes in good ways, as I have shared about my life in Kansas City. Sometimes other difficulties arise.

My sister, Evelyn, called on September 21st. She had seen our brother, John, the day before. He said, "Mom's getting worse. She is going outside late at night." Sometimes he or his wife, Gay, would find her outside, just staring off into space. Her mind was coming and going. Gay said that once she went to see mother and could smell gas before opening the door. In fact, she hesitated, thinking something might blow up. She found the gas burner on the stove turned on, but not lit, and mother asleep in her bed. This was, of course, very disconcerting to all of us. We moved mother to an assisted living apartment, where someone came by to help with food and personal assistance.

It was also on September 21st, that I spoke with Duane. He said, "I am sick of having AIDS." He was now on testosterone to help him gain weight. It was causing mood swings. He was taking huge amounts of pills. He then said, "I go to AA and AIDS support groups. Then I go home at night and I still have AIDS."

On the 26th, Duane called early in the morning to wish me, "Happy Birthday, Mother." Oh, how I miss all the wonderful celebrations we shared.

We spoke again on September 29th. Duane said he would be glad for me to come down. I would need to stay at a hotel, since the room with the futon is always hot or cold.

He had decided to stay in Houston for Thanksgiving and planned to go to his dad's for Christmas to see two of their girls, Lisa and Christie. He added, "I would like to come to Kansas City sometime."

Late in the afternoon of November 7th, I was in the lobby of our building, when Karen, our secretary said, "Elaine, you have a call." I answered, "Good afternoon. This is Elaine." All at once this precious voice said, "I'm feeling like a big baby, and I want my Mama."

Duane had just given himself his first shot and it had been quite an ordeal. I am not sure what the medication was, but he hadn't done this before. After talking for a few minutes, he was okay. I certainly understand because there have been many times in my life when I just wanted to hear my mother's voice. I was so happy that we were at this place in our relationship again.

After hanging up the phone, I wrote at the bottom of my note, "God–I love that kid–my darling child! He may think I was terrible at parenting, but when the rubber meets the road—he still wants "His Mama!" I'm sure God said, "I love him, too!"

When we talked one day in November, he said his dad was buying him some new tires before he got his car inspected. So, you see, in his own way, Duane's dad tried to show he cared.

He said he had been off the medication which was an opium derivative for a long time. He only used it five days and it made him throw up; he was also stoned out of his mind when on it. He ended our conversation with, "Well, Honey, I'm getting sleepy."

Yes, things were better between us. You can see how hard we both worked at this thing called a relationship between mother and son. You can also see why you don't want to do anything which could ever give you any kind of sexually transmitted disease. The pleasure derived is not worth the price you and your loved ones pay.

By the end of November 1994, his disease was a little more manageable. His shots seemed to be working. He was able to eat a lot more. He shared with me that he had visited with a girl he had dated a few times, but hadn't seen for a long time. He said, "I was able to talk with her openly and honestly."

I'm not sure he was still attending AA meetings at this time, but going through that program really did help him get honest with himself. We all know how difficult that is to do. I have the highest regard for the AA program.

I am always amazed at how good God is to all of us. If we just look for them, He sprinkles all kinds of blessings into our lives, even when some of our life is challenging.

The last part of November, I got a call asking me to speak at the first-ever International Wheat Summit. I tried to tell the man who called that as the National Sales Manager for Luzier Cosmetics; I was not qualified to talk about using wheat in cosmetics! I don't know who else had turned him down, but he wasn't going to take "no" for an answer. He said, "It is not so much about formulation. We want you to excite them about the prospect of thinking "wheat in cosmetics."

After I agreed to the request, I asked, "Now to whom am I going to be speaking?" He said, "farmers (I thought, okay), producers (okay), professors (I was getting worried), and bio-chemists (I was definitely out of my league)."

Did you catch the word, International? Did I tell you that I only graduated from high school? I really don't know why I didn't back out. I've been told more than once, that I like a challenge.

I called my old friend Bill Coats in Dallas, and he faxed me some information. I spoke with our cosmetic chemist. I did quick research. The Summit was held on December 8th, so I was on a fast track to put together an intelligent, amusing, 20 minute presentation.

When I shared my apprehension with Duane, he told me he really supported me. He then said, "I'm not surprised at your being asked. You are really good at what you do. They want your excitement and that is what you bring to any table or group." I guess I didn't sound totally convinced. I said, "Duane, these are heavy-hitters." To which he replied, "Mother, in your field, you are a heavy-hitter!" Long story short, I gave my presentation and it was a success.

To add to the pressure of the "Summit day," I was Chairperson of our Gladstone Chamber of Commerce Installation Banquet that night. Yes, it was quite an exciting day.

I had not planned to share this with you, but I know from my personal experiences of life, how important it is to believe in other people. We need to let them know we believe in them. Duane always knew I believed in him. I always knew my mother and daddy believed in me. Most of the things I have accomplished in life that have made me stretch, is because someone encouraged me.

They believed me to be more capable than I thought I was. An example was when I accompanied Bill Coats to Spain to train a company through an interpreter. I had never done such a thing, but he thought I could, so I did.

Of course, Duane was my number one "cheerleader", and then Dudley joined him. After Duane died, Dudley took over. I do miss them both, but do have things written from them.

Perhaps there is someone that you can reach out to today and say by word or action or both, "I believe in you!" You can be the difference in someone's life. Speak a blessing into their life. It might surprise you what can happen!

December was a rather smooth month for both of us. Duane had a nice trip to Dallas for Christmas. He had some quality time with his dad and Liz, as well as a couple of his friends. By this time in his life, he enjoyed each blessing which came to him.

1995 started out pretty rocky for Duane physically, but we were in a good place. Sometimes his mind worked in slow motion. Several of the drugs he was taking were like narcotics, slowing the body down, to help with the nausea and diarrhea.

At this time, he still carried the pneumonia that brought on his diagnosis of AIDS, plus a type of skin cancer, a kind of T.B., an eye problem that can cause blindness, and the intestinal problems continued. And, yes, he still wanted to live.

Duane had seen a movie which led him to say, "Ultimately you end up with whoever will stick by you. It is not always your choice and often it is not who you expect." For many years I had said, "I have not always been loved by the people I thought would love me. However, God has never left me without someone to love me and that I could love."

I think my ability to stick by someone to the end started with my parents. I saw my mother take such good care of my daddy the last months of his life. My son saw me stay to the end with my friend who died from AIDS. My husband, Dudley, saw me see Duane off to Heaven. Then, my sweet husband Dudley's mind was so mixed up and confused his last year or so. Yet six months before he died he said to me as we left his neurologist's office, "Elaine, when you commit to something, you see it through to the end."

Where do you think we get the strength to "be there for others"? It is all from the Lord. It is from the power of The Holy Spirit that lives inside all Christians. We just don't always let that power flow through us.

As Duane said, "On any given day, you do the best you can." I know so many people who are living with extreme health challenges. I hope whatever your situation is, this book will encourage you to look to God for comfort, strength, and love. He is always there waiting with open arms to embrace you.

I can't remember which friend took him, but Duane went to Graceland in Memphis in early 1995. On the 16th of March, we talked about the fact that he had a great trip, even though he did get tired.

It was about this time that he met Juan who would, besides me, stick with him all the way to death. He is the one I have already quoted. Like him, I pray this book will bring healing and forgiveness to many people, even where there is not agreement on every issue.

You may not understand what I am about to say. That's okay. Even though I did not want Duane in the homosexual lifestyle, I appreciated all Juan did for him. He gave up a lot for Duane. Juan expected to be in Houston for four years with his job. Duane said, "In four years I will be doing great or I will be dead." Neither of us ever ran from that reality.

During this long phone conversation about his new friend and his trip to Memphis, Duane said, "I am so lucky. I have good friends, a good roommate, a boyfriend, and parents who love me. I have a net, a great support system."

He went on to say, "I am so grateful. Today I feel good. I had money to go to a movie. I can buy a comic once in awhile. I'm not working. This is my retirement. You get what you get. I am trying to look at this as "my time."

He then spoke of a man in his group who had a bad attitude. He said, "He's an atheist. He thinks when he dies, that's it." You see, even when Duane was not sure what he believed, he really did believe. He just didn't want me to imply what he should believe. That's fair!

Duane then talked about having to be willing to say he needed help, then accepting help, and yes, asking for help. He talked about how good Juan was for him. His illness had taken such a toll on him by now. He said, "I felt like damaged merchandise. It is a real gift to see myself through Juan's eyes. He thinks I am beautiful, inside and out."

He continued, "I hope you won't feel guilty about your grief, or guilty if you can't get here. Knowing how you will be at the end, is **really important** to me."

Remember, at this time I lived in Kansas City and he was in Houston. We both knew something could happen quickly, and I might not be there. I loved and appreciated his attitude. However, God had a better plan. I was with him at the end and it was beautiful.

In April 1995, he saw a portion of the AIDS quilt. At that time, the entire quilt was the size of 17 football fields. I have never seen it. Duane said it was quite an experience. He visited with several families. He actually met the mother of someone he knew. He didn't say, but I would be willing to bet (if I did that sort of thing), he gave her a "big bear hug."

During the conversation about the quilt, Duane thanked me for some pictures, which were taken one day while he and his co-workers were climbing a pole for an exercise intended to create trust between them. Duane was afraid of heights, so this was a real fete on his part. I hoped it would remind him of how much he had already overcome.

He had talked for some time and he was emotional about his father and money. He said, "God can take care of the light bill and if He doesn't, it will be okay." I don't know if I sent money then or not. He was laboring with his words, so we said goodbye.

I watched a movie about divorce that night. I called Duane back and said, "Whatever sins you have committed, divorce is as bad, or worse. Please forgive me."

I said, "I want us to quit talking about your daddy. You should not have to be worrying about who will pay for your funeral." To be perfectly fair, his dad and Liz paid half of the expense for his cremation. My darling Dudley paid the other half and all the additional funeral expenses. I bought containers for the cremains, and he and I will share a niche in the columbarium in the Shepherd's Garden at Lovers Lane United Methodist Church.

The movie about divorce really touched me at an inner core. I couldn't get the movie off my mind. On April 17, 1995, I wrote the following poem for Duane.

THEY SAID

Twenty-five years ago...they said,
Don't worry about the children;
They adjust quickly, but they did not.
Quality time with your children,
Quality, not quantity is what
Your children will count;
But they did not.

It was quantity they wanted; their
little hearts yearned for hours;
Not quality of minutes. To them,
the precious little children,
Quantity seemed like quality; no
matter how the quantity was filled.

They said, if it feels good, do it.
If you are not with the one you love,
Love the one you are with.
Free love, it seems it was called.
But oh, what a price was paid for
what was advertised as free.

Let's see, there was divorce, alcoholism,
Lovers without faces and names,
And nightmares for memories.
But, oh, yes, FREE they were.
And what of the children?
Those precious little spirits.
Oh, yes, they adjusted,
But cope, they did not.

> They blotted out their pain by
> Drinking and smoking, and
> They even tried,
> That FREE love stuff.
> And what of the children?
> Today...AIDS is killing
> Those precious little children.
> Adjust? Oh yes; but cope, they did not.
>
> By the way...Where are THEY????
> I want to scream in their ears,
> And beat on their chests and say,
>
> Together...YOU and I KILLED,
> The children...
> The precious little children.

On May 2nd, 1995, we had a nice, long talk. He had been experiencing some incredible pain, which he thought was gas. He said, "I have a strong will to live. I have discovered when I get a shot; it is like a life force." He told me I needed to be good to Juan. He talked about Juan's spirituality. He finished the call by saying, "Yes, I know, you would be good to Juan." We both said, "I love you." And then goodbye.

May 15th, Duane called, "You are so sweet to me and love me so much, that if we had planned to spend $100 and I was looking at a $200 item, you would probably say, "Go ahead." He went on to say he didn't want me to be in a bind.

May 23rd was Duane's birthday. I called to wish him a Happy Birthday. The next day, he told me what a great day he had. His HIV lunch group of 14 people sang to him. He ran into people he hadn't seen for awhile. He and Juan had a nice dinner and watched a movie. Duane fell asleep for a bit, then walked Juan to the door. He said, "I had a great birthday." As I have said before, "What a great attitude!" What a fabulous son I had.

CHAPTER 6

Mother—the Only One I Can Trust

* * *

In June of 1995, Duane visited me in Kansas City. Everyone in the office was excited for me. For Mother's Day, he had called and talked with one of the girls who worked with me. She had given him the name of a local florist. He ordered this gorgeous bouquet of spring flowers in a beautiful container and sent them to me at the office. Of course everyone had heard all about Duane and how wonderful he was.

His doctor had warned me that he was quite thin. In fact, she suggested he send me a picture so I wouldn't be so surprised. She told him, "Your mother might not recognize you when you get off the plane and that would be difficult for both of you." He answered, "My Mother will know me!" Of course I knew him! His beautiful brown eyes were still bright and sparkling. His smile was the same warm, loving smile. Yes, his body was thin, but still beautiful to me.

Before he arrived, Duane and I had agreed not to discuss the homosexual lifestyle or anything that had to do with it. We had all kinds of plans. He was only there for three or four days. One day we went to the famous Country Club Plaza and shopped. It was fun to buy him a few new things.

On Saturday, the day before his departure, Duane just had to try one more time to sell me on the idea of same sex marriage. I didn't want to go there, but he pushed and pushed. (I know, some of you are saying, "Like mother, like son.") Yes, we are both strong in our convictions. I wanted to cave into him. I just couldn't tell him something was okay that the Bible did not affirm.

The difference between Duane and me was that I would have never tried to convince my mother of something that I knew she couldn't affirm. We had a difficult time that morning which ended in both of us crying. However, we pulled ourselves together and went for an enjoyable lunch. Then, thanks to a girl at the office who gave us tickets, we headed to a play.

Even though the day got off to a rocky start, we had a great day. I had given Duane my bed and I was sleeping on the couch. Of course, I'm a mom! After he went to bed, I heard him crying. I knocked on the door, and he invited me in. As I walked in, not knowing what to expect, I saw he was sitting on the end of the bed with a very sad look and tears flowing gently down his thin little face. I just wanted to die on the spot! But, no, I couldn't leave him.

He said, "I'm afraid. I am not afraid of dying, but I am afraid of getting from here to there."

I replied, "I am afraid for you. Anyone who knows anything about this disease would be afraid. I will promise you this. I will never abandon you. There is nothing you can say or do to cause me to leave you. I will walk right up to the door of death with you. I can't go through the door with you, but I know someone who can. You don't want to hear about Him right now" (meaning Jesus).

I went on to say, "Son, you know how much I love you, don't you?" He said, "Yes, Mother." I continued, "Well as much as I love you, I don't begin to love you as much as God loves you, because I don't know how to love like He does."

Wringing my hands, I said, "You know how much I want you to be in Heaven. God wants you there even more. I promise you that He isn't up there wringing His hands trying to figure out how to get you from here to there. He has a plan and He will take care of you all the way."

I had been standing right in front of him as he sat on the end of the bed. Suddenly he grabbed me, buried his head into my body, and said, "Mother, you are the only one I can trust!"

At that very instant it was like a light bulb came on inside my head and I thought, "if I had ever caved in one time, rather than standing on my Biblical beliefs, he couldn't trust me either."

We kissed and hugged and told each other over and over how much we loved the other. We were both pretty wrung out and I think he was glad to leave the next day to get back to Houston and Juan.

At that time in Duane's journey, he believed in God, but was confused about what he believed about Jesus. I have prayed for a lot of people but I have never prayed for anyone as much as I prayed for Duane to return to his faith in Jesus that he had as a child.

Something amazing happened to me that last night of Duane's visit. I had always known that God loves more than we do, but when I heard those words coming out of my mouth, that God loves Duane more than I do, it went into the deepest part of me. I really got that truth!

I was able to turn Duane over to God completely. No more trying to save him. No more trying to change him. I was leaving all that up to God. I was just going to love him and be there for him. I released him totally to God!

The last months of 1995 were another rather peaceful period for Duane and me. He was getting to know Juan, and was attending yoga classes which Juan conducted. He was also taking some Spanish classes. He and Juan were planning on going to Lima, Peru the first part of November. They would be gone for about two weeks.

I was concerned about his health issues, but didn't say much. Remember, I had given him to God. I was doing my best to live out that decision. He was beginning to say, "I love you" first, instead of it being a response to my saying it. We were in a more relaxed relationship.

I had been to an exhibit of the "Treasurers of the Czars" and purchased a tee shirt for him with that logo. He was excited about his little gift. These were small steps, but Duane and I were beginning to revert back to our former way of relating to each other.

In October he ran a fever for two weeks, but the trip to Peru was still on track for the first of November. I found a note saying he was leaving on November 5, 1995. By the time he left Houston, his fever was gone. That was a relief for both of us.

After Duane announced he was going to Peru, I thought, "Gee, what if he gets over there and gets sick or even dies?" I needed a new passport if I was to go to him. I found you can get a passport quickly if you want to pay extra for it, which I did.

When my sweet mother heard that Duane was going to Peru, she wanted to give him a little money to spend. She needed help in getting it to him in a hurry, so on 10-31-95 I sent him by FedEx $50 from his grandmother. She was 88 years old at the time and in my eyes, almost perfect. That was a lot of money to her, but it was her way of expressing love for Duane.

It was good that my job kept me so busy. I was in a different city nearly every weekend from the end of July to the middle of November. I would leave on Thursday and return on Sunday.

I usually had dinner with the local managers on Thursday night. I held a managers' meeting on Friday and an all day general conference for all our salespeople on Saturday. Saturday night was my time to collapse. I would go to my hotel room, order room service, and chill out.

The company never complained because I was very frugal with my expense account. I didn't drink alcohol or order expensive meals. I loved my work, and Luzier had wonderful people working for them.

As a side note, I was in Dallas in September of 1995 on a business trip. While there, I went to see my friend, Sally Dancer, Dudley's wife, at her place of business. You may remember that Sally had cancer. She looked really good that day. In fact, someone said later that I took one of the last pictures of her. We had a lovely visit, and she suggested I call Dud for lunch.

As I recall, Dudley and I mostly talked about Sally and Duane's illnesses and how brave they both were. Dud looked very tired and rather thin. Sally was able to work, but Dudley did most everything else. At the time he was the Pastor in charge of Congregational Care at Lovers Lane United Methodist in Dallas. It was a large church, and Dudley was responsible for hospital visits, home visits, and memorial services. How he kept from losing his health totally was a miracle. He never regretted giving Sally the wonderful care he gave her. It was good to catch up with my old friends.

Duane returned from Peru and called me almost immediately. It had been a good trip. While in Peru, he walked quite a lot. He experienced some of his now familiar problems, including nausea and diarrhea. He said the people of Peru were wonderful to him; very friendly and warm. He had learned some Spanish and was surprised that so many of them barely spoke Spanish there. Most children probably had only a fifth grade education. Like so many foreign countries, lots of children were begging on the streets.

Duane said he couldn't live there because of his health, but he was glad he went. I was relieved when he sat foot back in the good old USA!

On December 3rd, we had another one of those long conversations where I took copious notes. We talked about his financial needs. Again, he had dying on his mind.

He said, "I would love for Uncle Dud to conduct a Dallas service." He asked for *Amazing Grace* and *Softly and Tenderly Jesus is Calling* to be sung. He continued, "That was a good memory from First Baptist Dallas." He also wanted an opportunity for people to speak. We did that in Houston. Dudley and I spoke in Dallas. I am sure he liked what we said. Dudley wrote him a poem.

As we continued talking, Duane said, "I believe God has protected me all my life. I am grateful to God. He provided me such a good life in spite of all I did. I drove drunk for sixteen years. I didn't get hurt and I didn't hurt anyone else. The night I got shot, I could have been paralyzed or I could have died. I couldn't have gotten off cocaine and alcohol without God. I lost my job. Now I only have eleven thousand dollars a year. Instead of doing drugs, I got sober."

As you can see, he was getting very real with me. He said, "I had been up all night doing drugs. We had the mattress in the middle of the floor. I was exhausted. Dad called at 2:00 p.m. in the afternoon. I couldn't talk. I thought, "Here my Dad is calling and I am so messed up I can't talk to him." That event brought me to the place where I wanted to be sober."

So, Jim, if he felt you never gave him your love, he wanted your love so badly he got sober; not immediately, but that was the beginning. I thank you!

He talked more about his memorial service. He knew his health was becoming more compromised all the time. Like we always had done, we were talking about everything. I do miss him so!

Duane continued, "I don't disbelieve in Jesus Christ. I just don't know what I believe. I have known good Christians and a lot of not so good Christians. I have had some bad experiences."

I suppose most of us could say the same thing. I have often said that Jesus has never offended anyone, but lots of people have been offended in the name of Jesus. Some of you may feel that way as you read this book. I pray you will not, but don't blame Jesus, please. Perhaps you might open His book, the Bible, and read for yourself God's love letter to you. You just might be surprised.

Duane wasn't finished with our conversation. "You know the book, *Men From Mars, Women From Venus?* I am sort of from Jupiter. I am a man, but was raised to think like a woman. I get mad as hell at you. Losing control is bad. I know when I am going to lose control. When I get mad at you it matters. Nothing hurts me so much as to see you cry, especially if I am the reason."

He wasn't through with me yet. Apparently from my notes, I said nothing. I just listened. He needed that. He needed for me to really hear him. Duane continued. "I told you I was gay because I wanted to be honest with you. When you reacted the way you did, I think I felt betrayed. You had said I could tell you anything. I thought I had made a mistake telling you. I went to a bar and got drunk. I don't like confrontations. I walk away. I am not blaming you for my alcoholism. I was called a fagot as a boy and got beat up. Dad didn't want a relationship with me and you didn't approve of me. I was on cocaine for a year and a half. Last night I couldn't just eat a little ice cream. I ate a huge bowl. I can't do a little bit. It is not in my nature to buy one polo shirt. I buy five of them. Alcohol is different from cocaine. With cocaine, less than 3% are able to stay sober. Your brain thinks it has to have cocaine. It has been two and a half years since I have done anything. It doesn't even occur to me. I don't even go to AA anymore. Last night I picked up a bottle and put it away." I guess that belonged to his roommate, Tom. Duane didn't say.

I am exhausted writing all this. Bet you are exhausted reading it. I hope it gives some of you the courage to continue the process of loving someone who may not always feel loving towards you.

CHAPTER 7

Surprised by Love

* * *

As we turn the pages of the calendar to a new year, I suppose we all wonder what the year will bring. I have never been really big on making New Year's resolutions. On the first day of January, 1996, there was no way for me to imagine what a glorious year this was going to be for me. Yes, even in spite of my precious son's illness, what surprises were in store for me!

I did speak with Duane that day. He was eating cookies as we talked. He said, "I am so lucky." Since Juan was in New York, and Tom was leaving for London, Duane had asked if he could borrow $40. Tom had thrown him his ATM card to use. He had gotten $60 and said to me, "I will be okay until I get my check."

I am so proud of Duane. He had learned how to live on very little. He spent a great deal of energy and time in finding new drug sources. He had been sick with a cold or anemia much of December. He had found a medication for anemia, but it was quite expensive. He had gotten a blood transfusion the previous Saturday. That always gave him more energy. Once someone has AIDS, they have less energy and yet it takes a lot of energy to stay alive.

Juan was coming home the next day. They had met one year ago. Duane ended our conversation by saying, "Considering I didn't think I would see 1996, 1995 was wonderful!" Then we each said, "I love you." What a great way to start the New Year together.

By the end of the month, Duane was in the hospital for a few days. He was on a medication which forces the bones to produce white blood cells. This causes great pain. He also was very nauseated again.

Duane continued to fight hard. Even though he was having trouble breathing, was experiencing some fever, and coughing up blood occasionally, the one time he left the house was to go to a Spanish class. How neat is that! He did raise the bar on how to live! At least his bones were not hurting so much.

We spoke on the ninth of February. In AIDS patients, they watch numbers called Viral Lode. You want low numbers. At this time, Duane's was off the chart; 250,000 is high; Duane's was over 5 million. You can see why I sing the praises for his doctor and Duane. They investigated every medicine they could find to keep him going.

On the 10th, Duane was having a very bad day. He was hurting all over again. On top of that, he threw up everything he ate. One good thing happened. Juan had sold Duane's car, which gave him a little cash. I was so proud of Duane. He made the decision about giving up driving. I don't remember the exact date, but he just said rather casually, that he didn't feel he should be driving anymore. I pray I will be so graceful about giving over my car keys.

I made a note on the 28th saying I had cried for one and a half hours. I wrote, "I hurt so badly that you are ill and I can do nothing about it." I felt so alone and so far away. I was comforted knowing that Duane had Juan in his life to care about him. I had just returned from Nashville that day, traveling for Luzier again. I was gone a couple of weekends a month. It was good for me.

From time to time, we would go over end-of-life measures. He didn't want extraordinary measures taken. We were never sure about the feeding part. You will see at the end of his life how God took care of that for us. Duane talked about the fact his life had been good and interesting. He felt God had blessed him. He was just getting tired of the pain. He said he didn't want to hurt and was hoping we could stop the pain. I do hope you will have these conversations with your loved ones. It makes it so much easier on everyone at the end of life.

Duane's relationship with his father was improving by this time. Jim was calling him about once a week to check on him. I am sure he had no idea how much Duane appreciated this.

One day in April, Duane called saying, "I wanted to check on you. I didn't want you to feel brushed off." Evidently, I had called and he had to run, so said goodbye quickly. He went on to say that I was doing the right thing to take care of my job and myself.

He said, "I know how you feel about me being so sick and facing death. I cried when I received a call telling me about dad's recent health scare. I had dealt with the concept of my dying but had not dealt with the possibility of Dad dying." This experience seemed to give him a new understanding for how difficult his disease was for us, his parents.

During April, I was in Dallas on business. While there, a friend approached me about a job I might enjoy with her company. I decided I would pursue it, in order to be closer to Duane. Upon returning to Kansas City I spoke to Keith about leaving Luzier. He said, "Well, we don't want to lose you. If you need to be in Dallas, we can just move you back there." He even offered to rent an apartment in Houston where I could work one or two weeks a month. I told him that wasn't necessary. He was wonderful to me.

While things were getting back to our old, wonderful, and normal loving ways between Duane and me, life was not good for his Aunt Sally and Uncle Dud.

Sally had lived longer than the doctors expected when she was diagnosed with her cancer, but she was getting weaker. On May 2, 1996, she left her family and went into the arms of Jesus. It was, of course, very difficult for her family and friends. She had lots of people who loved her.

Dudley's secretary, Suzanne, was a rock for Dudley. I had spoken with her occasionally when I called Dud about Sally or to report on Duane. She said Dudley had lots of support, so even though we had been friends a long time, it wasn't necessary for me to be at the memorial service.

On May 20th, Duane called me at work, leaving a message that he had some exciting news. He had gotten approved for a new drug. It had not only stopped the progression of the disease for some, but had reversed some of the bad results of AIDS. Truly, like his mother, he was an eternal optimist.

When Duane and I talked on the 23rd for his birthday, he said, "I was up at 4:45 a.m. this morning. I had a great conversation with God. Then I wrote to my dad on his Father's Day card. I went for a haircut and afterwards Tom took me to lunch. A guy is coming over to build shelves for my comics and Tom is paying for half of the cost for my birthday. Tonight Juan and I are going to the theatre."

I moved back to Dallas the July 4th weekend. The end of June I had found an apartment, with the help of some friends.

When I got settled in, I called Dudley to see how he was doing. He called several times when he was having a bad day. Once he had been working in Sally's flowerbed and started crying. He needed someone to listen as he worked through his feelings.

We went to dinner a couple of times. I was very nervous about going, as I was afraid people would talk, since Sally had just died.

Duane said, "Mother, go. You are two old friends having dinner."

The first time we went, I made Dudley wait until much later in the evening. I sat pulling at my skirt all during our meal. I thought it was too short to be wearing with a preacher.

One day Dudley said, "I am going to call one of these days when I am not having a bad time."

My reply was, "Dudley, you have been there for me so many times over the years when I was having a rough time. I am just glad I can be here for you."

As Dudley and I spent more time together, our deep abiding friendship turned into a wonderful love. We couldn't tell you the date, but we both knew the moment we knew we were in love. What a sweet experience.

Duane was so pleased that I was having a good time with his Uncle Dud. He knew it had been a long time since I had cared for anyone. The first time Dudley mentioned the "M" word (yes, marriage) I said, "The church will never approve of my past." His reply was very simple, "The church doesn't have to know about your past. I know all about it and it doesn't scare me at all."

It was true. He had been my very special confidant over the years, so he did know everything about me. In fact, he admired me for where I had been and how I had persevered. His faith in me made me want to be a better person.

Even though Dudley and I were spending a lot of time together, we were both still very involved with our families.

I was talking to Duane several times a week. During August, he felt pretty tired most of the time. I don't remember how he got connected to the church, but he started attending the First Unitarian Universalist Church. He found great acceptance there. They told him there were many windows to God and he could find his own way to God.

That was not the church I would have chosen for him, but God knew Duane could find his way back to Jesus in that church. By that time in our relationship, I knew not to be negative, and my response was sincere, as well as wise. I simply said, "I am so happy you have found a place you can enjoy."

God knows so much more than we do. It has been my experience that God rarely works like we think He will. I try so hard to stay out of His way now.

It was at this time Duane had a line put in his arm for a permanent IV. He was taking medication twice a day for the CMV in his eyes. The process to administer the medication took one hour each time. He was blessed they had discovered the CMV, because undetected, it caused blindness. Are you beginning to see how difficult controlling all the symptoms of AIDS was becoming? Yet, he stated, "I am not dying, I just feel really bad, just yucky." Even so, he asked about my trip.

I had gone to Oklahoma to see Mother. We had a big gathering at Evelyn's and Dave's church, the place where I went to church as a child. The old building was gone, but many of the people were the same. I remember talking to my nephew, Steve, and his wife, Gayle, about Dudley and me. They encouraged us not to wait if we decided we loved each other.

As life would have it, I am glad we didn't put off getting married. Because of Dud's Parkinson's, we only had nine and a half years together. The first eight years were terrific, and then his disease began to progress pretty rapidly.

By the end of August, Duane's CMV was completely dormant. They were able to drop his medication to once a day. He and Juan were able to go to Las Vegas the middle of September for training for a travel service they were going to pursue. This gave Duane a new project and a way to feel productive again.

I was still traveling for Luzier. It was as though we were all in a three ring circus. I was talking to Duane and Dudley a lot. I still loved my job and things were going well.

Once I came home from a trip to find that Dudley had prepared dinner for me. It was so nice to have someone being so good to me. It didn't change Duane's illness, but at least, I finally had someone who could actually share my pain.

We had set November 16th as our wedding date. Duane was so pleased he could make reservations for Evelyn and Dave and Pat and Norman, my sisters and brothers-in-law to come for our big day.

We had gotten everyone's approval, including our children, our mothers, and, yes, the church. Thanks to Steph, we had rings and my dress had been purchased.

We were so excited, and then we had a bit of a let down. I talked to Duane the evening of October 24th, only to hear that he was down from 119 to 102 pounds. He said, "I am dropping away. We are going to try Marinol next week. I didn't do well with it before, but we have to try something." He continued saying, "I'm okay. I'm at peace about this. I am so grateful for Uncle Dud. It is okay for me to go now. Sunday I was going to church, but I just couldn't go. I thought if I can't go, why fight it?"

When we talked on the 29th, he said his doctor was very concerned about his weight. He had decided not to stay on the Marinol, as it put him to sleep. They were considering TPN, which is intravenous nutrition. He was to see the doctor the next day.

When I asked him if he was still thinking of coming to the wedding, he said, "In case I can't, can you come down before you marry?" I asked about coming that weekend. Quickly he said, "Please, I would like for you to come." He went on to say that he wanted me to stay at his apartment. You can see how far our relationship had come.

Before saying goodbye, he said, "Last night I woke up at 3:00 a.m...I couldn't sleep because my legs hurt so badly. I told Tom that if my mother was here, she would rub my legs and talk me to sleep." He was so right! Even now, I sob as I write. My, how I loved that boy!

How grateful I am that God chose me to be his Mother. How grateful I am that God gave me the physical, emotional, and spiritual strength to endure, to be there for him all the way to Heaven. Oh, Father God, how I love You. Jesus, thank You for dying for all our sins. Sweet Holy Spirit, thank You for being my personal guide through all of this.

Duane and his doctor decided to go with the TPN for at least two weeks. "I'm really hoping this will make a big difference," he said, "It will help or I'll die. I'm slipping away."

As I write, I think of all of you who have loved ones who are slipping away either physically like Duane was, or mentally like my precious Dudley did a few years later.

I never want to sound like I think we had it any harder than you have had it. Maybe you are experiencing something similar now. I feel your pain and I am sorry you have to suffer. Perhaps you can let your tears flow now.

Duane was having a lot of rough nights. One night he awoke about 3:30 a.m. He said that his whole nervous system was going crazy; that every nerve in his body was tingling. To get relief he had taken 5 sleeping pills. As thin as he was and as weak as he was, it was a miracle he didn't accidentally kill himself. He said, "I am really looking forward to seeing you Saturday."

I went for a couple of days. We had a very nice time together. We were finally so okay with each other. We were mother and son, so full of love for the other. I want to encourage all of you who are struggling with a child in any way. Keep loving, keep praying, keep talking, and keep on believing.

Here are a few of Duane's remarks after that weekend.

"I enjoyed having you here."

"Thank you for all you did."

"I loved my time with you."

"I'm worried about you. It is important for you to get your married life started right. I don't want to interfere."

"I won't come to the wedding if it will be too hard for you." (I guess he thought I would be sad about his illness.)

"I love feeling a part of the family."

The next day, he went to the doctor. The new line for his TPN didn't work. He had a high fever for two days. In a couple of days they were going to put in a central line. Even feeling badly, he went to vote. Oh how I admired him!

Duane was an example of how even though we sometimes do things to mess up our life, God can turn our life around and use us for an example to many others. He was always a wonderful person, but he soared to new heights those last two years of his life.

Sometimes we all feel like we have gone too far down a path for good to ever come of it, but sometimes our mistakes are what lead us to our greatest achievements! Stay strong, don't give up!

You can see that Duane and I talked a lot about his dying. One day he said, "If you need to give me something, Demoral is good for me…I go to la la land and wake up happy. Try to make my path easy. Most of us finally die from malnutrition. As far as a memorial service, I'm okay with whatever you want to do. I'm tired; there is nothing left unsaid or undone."

When they put in Duane's central line, it took them 45 minutes to stop the bleeding. Then they took him to be X-rayed and the blood started pouring out again. They did more stitches, X-rayed him and sent him home in a wheel chair.

What a super guy he was. It was about this time that he said, "I'm a business man again. I think I am going to love this job." He was referring to his new travel pursuit.

After speaking about my wedding numerous times, Duane decided he better not try to come. We were both disappointed, but knew he was struggling to survive.

He kept telling me that this was an answer to his prayers for me. He had been worried about how I would be when he was gone. Once he told me, "I not only approve, I am not just relieved, I am happy for you and Dud. I think this is a wonderful situation."

Dudley and I decided to change our plans for a trip. We would go to Houston to see Duane first, then to the Hill Country just outside San Antonio. On November 13th, just three days before our wedding, Duane and I talked about our time in Houston. He was feeling better. In fact, the TPN was working. He had gained 10 pounds in two weeks but he was short of breath, so they had given him a blood transfusion.

We made plans to go to lunch with Juan one day, and dinner with Larry, Duane's former partner one night. Larry still calls me Mom and I love it, because I love him. Yes, they all know that I wish they were not living that lifestyle, but it doesn't keep me from loving them. Just because I can't affirm someone's behavior doesn't mean I don't affirm them. We are not, any of us, our behavior. After talking through our plans, Duane ended by saying, "I could spend every minute with you, but this is your wedding trip."

On November 16, 1996, Dudley and I were married in a quiet, sweet ceremony in Wesley Chapel. We were surrounded by our families and a few of our closest friends. We spent our first night together at the Dallas Renaissance

Hotel. It was a lovely suite, and it was wonderful to be husband and wife at this time in our lives.

The next day we drove to Houston, we saw Duane, and then checked into the Renaissance Hotel there. We lunched with Duane and Juan the next day.

After a couple of nights alone, Dud reserved a room adjoining our suite for Duane to come and join us. Dudley always said one of his greatest memories was waking up about 3:00 a.m. and hearing Duane and I giggling in the next room as we ordered room service! What a great Dad he was to Duane! How blessed we were!

Dud, Elaine and Duane

At the time, we knew what Dudley brought to me and Duane. Dud healed all the pain of my past hurts over men. He gave Duane the fatherly love he had always longed for.

We didn't understand to the fullest extent all that I brought to Dudley. He used to say, "Elaine, you have fulfilled all my dreams and fantasies."

We loved doing ministry together. I loved being a wife to him in every sense of the word. Then, later, when Sarah was born, there were times Stephanie, like all new mothers, needed a mom figure. I loved being there for her. Of course, when Dud's Parkinson's disease got really bad, I could help the children with their daddy. As it turned out, Dudley brought to me and Duane what we needed, and I brought to their family what they needed. God was very good to all of us!

It was about this time that Duane first mentioned Shahn, his therapist for the last two years of his life. She was wonderful! After a few months, she and I became friends. I will tell you more about that later.

Duane wanted very much to come home to Dallas for Christmas to be with our family. He said, "I already feel such a part of this family."

Duane continued that day, saying, "I am so grateful that God has blessed me like this." Then he started crying, as he said, "I'm overwhelmed by Dud's love. This could have been my life for 33 years. I'm so grateful." He made that same statement many times over the next two years! He so loved and appreciated Dudley, who soon became just "Dad."

During one of our calls in December, he said, "It may be time for you to call my doctor and lobby for me to come to Dallas for Christmas." Her hesitation was that leaving him on the TPN for extended periods made infection likely. I did call her, as he asked.

I told her, "This may be my last Christmas with him and he wants to come home." She allowed it, because she trusted me. After all, I had trusted her with my most precious possession, my beloved son! They shipped the TPN in dry ice and we managed.

Shortly before Christmas, Duane and I talked. His roommate was thinking of moving out. Duane said, "I can live alone now. I couldn't six months ago. I have a tremendous will. I am not going to be defeated. I got my will from you. Thank you for making it possible to handle this with dignity. I know you love me. You are my best friend. It was worth all the hell we went through to get to this place. Thank you for my life and my character. We just didn't give up. I got that from you." Those words were like music to my ears. Hang in there, everyone. It is worth it!

Another day we were talking about Stephanie expecting and he said, "I'm an Uncle!" He loved that role.

Even though Duane's health was very tenuous, we were so thankful he felt like coming to Dallas for Christmas. We had some really wonderful times. The Dancer celebration at our house, with Duane being able to give everyone some nice gifts, gave him a great deal of satisfaction. We had a beautiful tree, lots of laughter, hugs, and "I love you" talks.

Duane especially loved being with Stephanie and Mike, because he had so many memories of his times with them over the years. It was good to be together as a family. Duane needed that so much.

I can still see Duane sitting on the couch with a large pan beside him, in case he had to throw up. Instead, all at once, his nose started bleeding. I helped him stop the bleeding, but he cleaned it up with bleach. Those were the instructions from the doctor. They thought the virus died when exposed to air, but it was better to be safe than sorry.

Duane and I had a couple of tense moments, but his visit went well. Later he shared with me that he and Juan had a little tiff the night before. He then stated, "I'm overly sensitive. Since there are so few things I can do, I'm very sensitive about anything that seems like criticism." Feeling totally out of control is a terrible feeling. Truthfully, if we admit it, none of us like to be criticized.

Duane and I were talking most every day now, if only for a few minutes. We kept working on our relationship; not so much the present, but the past.

As an example, on January 20th, 1997, I said, "I didn't want to go back to selling Sarah Coventry jewelry after my hysterectomy. Your dad panicked. He needed me to work, so he could leave."

Duane replied, "Oh, do you have any idea what you have just told me? I thought you wanted a career. I wanted you home at night to cook for me."

I then explained that I had gotten involved with Sarah Coventry as a fun thing, but was good at it and I was very competitive, so it got to be more than I wanted. I told him that as I lay in bed those long weeks, recovering from that difficult surgery, I decided that wasn't what I wanted to do with my life.

Looking back, I thank God that I had that work, not only to provide Duane and me with a living, but to prepare me for the rest of my jobs, which prepared me for being a good wife to Dudley.

Truly, all things do work together for good for those of us who love the Lord and are called according to His purpose. Yes, that is from the Bible. Check out Romans 8:28.

Duane and I talked about my working again those last two weeks of his life. He had told me earlier that he had resented me, but he forgave me. As a child, he never realized that I had to work in order for us to live.

As he got older, he was quite proud of me and what I had accomplished with my life. He will really be proud when I finally get this book written. I am sure you know how hard it is to put all of this "out there" for all of you to read.

The old folks used to say, "Don't air your dirty laundry in public." I don't like doing that, but if it can help one person, or one family, it is worth it. Besides, Duane told me to go educate the world.

One day as we spoke, Duane said, "What someone else thinks about me is none of my business. So what?" I thought you might like to ponder that a bit.

CHAPTER 8

Other Family Issues

* * *

We had to put my mother in a nursing home in February 1997. My sister, Evelyn had been so good to mother, but she called me and said, "You are going to have to come tell her she is going to the nursing home." I understood how hard it would be for everyone, so I went.

After thanking mother for taking such good care of us, I told her it seemed best for her to move to Medical Lodge. I tried to avoid the phrase nursing home.

One night soon after I had gone to Oklahoma to tell mother the news, Duane called me. He said, "It just occurred to me how hard that was for you to put your mother in a nursing home." He continued, "You had long talks with your mother. I know you will miss that. I can't take her place, but you can call and say you are missing your mother." Wasn't that sweet of my boy?

He told me that Juan was going to stay in Houston, although he had an offer to move and get a big raise. Juan said he wouldn't go without Duane. At this point, Duane needed to stay in Houston where his good doctor was. He was too sick to go somewhere else. He had also developed quite a wonderful relationship with some women at his church. He had three people who came every week to take him wherever he needed to go. Without Juan and the church friends, he couldn't have stayed in Houston the last part of his life. God did bless us so.

If you listen closely to people, they will tell you how they are growing spiritually. Duane's roommate was moving out of Houston and he didn't know how he was going to pay the rent. On February 4th, he called to say, "We need to trust in God. He just does so much better than we can ever imagine." Another young man, Jon, had agreed to move in to share the expenses of the apartment. "If I live another six months, I have had a nice place to live. I am excited and really grateful!"

By this time, Duane fought lots of pain in his back, his legs, and his feet. When we talked he would tell me about going to the doctor for this or that pain, but never in a complaining or whining way, just informative. He tried it all; different medications, yoga, electric shock, and even homeopathic methods. What was it going to hurt? Occasionally, something helped.

Duane was working a little with his travel agency business. It gave him a little extra money, and a sense of accomplishment. He was always generous with his time and his money.

One day he told me that every couple of months he gave to St. Joseph's Indian School. He explained it was a Christian school for poor Indian children. He said, "They get Christian exposure there. I'm not able to do a lot, but I do a little. I am so grateful for what I have." I continue giving to them in honor of Duane.

By March, Duane was really enjoying his church and the women who were serving so beautifully as caregivers. One of the ladies, Carol, had a little boy that she often brought with her. I was concerned that somehow he might be exposed through Duane's vomiting, nose bleeds, or diarrhea, but his mother was not concerned. As far as I know, God did protect the little guy. Duane loved both Carol and her son.

Another Duane quote from March was, "When people stop believing in God, they will believe in anything."

Yes, he was finding his way back to the faith of his childhood. It was a slow, thoughtful process. That same day he said, "It is okay for you not to work. I really love to be able to call and say, "Come down and spend a couple of days."

Over the next two years, if we hadn't seen Duane for two or three weeks, Dud would say, "Why don't you go check on our son?" That was music to my ears!

Easter was lovely that year. Duane enjoyed his time at his church. Dudley and I had a great day. Check out the picture below. It is one of my favorites.

Pastor Dudley and his Bride

One day Duane said, "I told everyone at church that my mother had worked so hard for so long. Now it is time for her to enjoy herself." He went on to say what an incredible blessing his church was to him. God does do good work!

I did give up my job with Luzier in April. I loved having more time with Dudley, Duane, and my Dancer children. I was finally living my dream with a man who was truly my "knight in shining armor."

For many years I had been out front, winning sales awards, receiving accolades, and then I was managing those who did the same. Now, I wanted to do nothing more than support and promote Dudley's ministry.

By April, Duane was not doing well. His eyes were yellowing, he was sleeping too much, and his blood cultures were growing bacteria. He said, "I want you to come down. I hate to take you away from Dad, but I would love to be with you." I think he was frightened. He said, "It may be my central line. There is a different one called Hickman." Although it is more expensive, he did get it later. I did go for a couple of days.

About this time one of my new friends at the church pulled me aside and told me she thought Dudley might have Parkinson's disease. She recognized some of the signs because her husband had the disease.

With Dudley, it was that rigid shoulder stance, the lack of facial expression, and the smaller writing. I had not been around Parkinson's, so I had just thought Dud was tired from caring for Sally on top of his demanding job.

We consulted Dr. Gary Tunell with Texas Neurology. That was one of the best decisions we ever made. Dr. Tunell is extremely knowledgeable and is a very kind man.

Even though we lost Dudley to the disease, Dr. Tunell was able to give us several wonderful years. He truly loved Dudley.

My life was very full and happy. I am grateful that even in the midst of sadness, I can usually enjoy the happy times God gives me. Dudley and I simply loved being married. Stephanie was about to give us our first granddaughter. Even though Duane struggled physically, he was so happy to be Dudley's son. I spent a lot of time driving back and forth to Houston.

May 2nd, 1997, our granddaughter Sarah was born! Dudley and I were at the hospital. Zenon was in the birthing room with Stephanie. She didn't want us with her. It was not that easy, but we didn't know there was a problem. We were visiting with other families who were waiting. All at once, I turned to Dudley, and said, "We've got to pray...RIGHT NOW!!" We did and a few minutes later Zenon came and told us that it had been scary, but that Sarah was here and she was fine.

He proceeded to say that Steph's doctor had said, "The baby is in distress. You have one minute, then we are going to have to go in and take her. Now...PUSH!" As near as we can figure, that was exactly the time I said, "We've got to pray!" Only God knew what was going on and somehow He let us be a part of it, even from the other room. How Great is our God!

Can you even begin to imagine how absolutely hysterically happy I was? I had wanted more children, but couldn't have them. Then my only son is living the gay lifestyle. I never thought I would be a grandmother. What I didn't know then, was that there would be a second darling granddaughter, Rachel, who would come into our lives two and a half years later.

Duane was overjoyed when I called him. He knew how much I wanted a grandbaby. He was thrilled for all of us and so excited to be an uncle.

Duane began to really struggle more physically by May. I was visiting every couple of weeks, just to give him emotional support.

It was during this time God helped me develop the art of "being present where you are." When I was in Houston, I was fully there. When I was in Dallas, I was fully here. It wasn't that I forgot about the rest of my family; I still prayed and called. However, my focus was on the people I was with at any given time.

That was a wonderful gift from God. I wasn't even aware of what was happening at first. I encourage all of us to remember to focus on the people where we are!

Even though Duane was not always doing well, he kept up the fight. On May 19th, he said, "I ordered dad's Father's Day gift. It is too large to wrap. You can take it back when you come down. I am so excited that you are coming soon."

A matinee date at the opera

Mother's Day was special for me that year. I'm quite sure we made a fuss over Stephanie, since this was her first Mother's Day. It was also she and Mike's first Mother's Day without their mother, Sally.

For me, I was so very happy to have my son loving me as he did all those years before everything got crazy in our lives. He sent me this wonderful book entitled, *MOTHERS [and] SONS*, by Mariana Cook. The pictures are fabulous and the words of the subjects are so special. The most special words are what Duane wrote on the inside front cover. He wrote, "Mother, I am so grateful for the good times that we have been able to share together this year. I look forward to talking with you every day, and miss you when I don't. God has blessed our lives in so many ways, and I know He will continue to do so." "With all my love, Your Son, Duane"

Tonight I opened this book to copy what he had written. I found another Mother's Day card from 1988. The card read, "I've always been so proud that you're my mother. Even when I was small, I could tell that you were pretty special. You never talked down to me. You were firm when you had to be and the rest of the time you were really fun to be with…It's no wonder I've always been so proud of you. And as the years go by, that pride is a feeling that just keeps on growing. Happy Mother's Day With All My Love.

Then Duane wrote, "I thought I would never find the right card for you—most of them are so trite. But this expresses my feelings perfectly! I always have been the very proudest of sons, and I always will be. You are the most exceptional mother, woman, and person that I have ever known! I love you so much! (I'm about to cry!) Duane.

Do you see why we were both so determined to get through the rough years (about two or three years of really high mountains and rugged terrain) to get back to this kind of love? The turnaround all started in Kansas City when he said, "You are the only one I can trust."

My Mother's Day was not over yet. I got a second package with another book entitled, *LIFE with MOTHER* by the

Editors of Life Magazine. Again, they are outstanding pictures. However, what made the gift so special was the inscription Duane penned.

He wrote, "Mother's Day comes twice this year. I hope you will find this book as moving as I have. I love you more than I can say. I know you understand, because I know you feel the same about me." Forever "Your Baby" I'll Be, Duane.

This was special because there was a time he didn't want me calling him Baby. It isn't that I had a deep need to call him that; it just meant that I could relax and be myself.

June was exciting for Duane. His cousin, Becky, whom he did not know very well, came from Florida to see him. My brother, Robert was a career Army officer, and his family had always lived some distance from us. If they visited Mother, I always made an effort to go see them.

Becky had flown through Houston in March and Duane had missed connecting with her after a mix-up with the airlines. He had gone to the airport in his wheelchair to see her, but missed her plane.

The wife of my nephew, Steve, wrote the airline about the situation. Thanks to Gayle's business expertise and the airline's kindness, Becky got a special fare back to Houston. She came for a weekend, arriving on June 6th. She and Duane asked me to join them for the weekend.

We had a great time and Duane and Becky really connected on a deep level. We watched the story of St. Frances of Assisi and I would catch them looking at each other as though they were seeing into each other's souls. It was quite beautiful to watch, but sometimes I almost felt like I was intruding. I felt it would have broken the moments to get up and leave. I don't think either of them knew I was there anyway.

One night we went to a Cajun place for dinner. Adjoining was a club with a dance floor. We all liked music and Duane and

I had danced together many times over the years. He was very frail, with a pain pump hanging over one shoulder, and had on flip-flops because his feet were so sore.

After a few minutes, he wanted us to dance. I was a little nervous, because he had been so ill, but I thought if he dies on the dance floor, okay. He would be doing something he loved to do...dance with his mother!

If I remember right, people just moved to the edge of the floor and a lot of them just watched us dance. I can't remember for sure, they may have even applauded when we finished the dance. To my knowledge, that is the last time he danced. I am so glad his sweet cousin, Becky, was there to experience his wonderful personality that weekend. Thanks Gayle, for making that all possible for all of us. Acts of kindness are never forgotten. What have you done for someone lately?

CHAPTER 9

My Reality for Now

* * *

In June Duane said, "I am beginning to experience some HIV dementia. I don't dwell on it. It doesn't happen all the time."

It was about this time he began to shrug his shoulders and say, "Oh well, this is my reality for now." We all so admired him and his attitude. Dudley and I used that phrase as his Parkinson's began to progress. As I have said before, but bears repeating, "Duane and Dudley raised the bar on how to live with debilitating diseases."

Sometimes when you think life can't get much worse, it does! Duane started running extremely high fevers and was anemic. He ended up spending all of July, with the exception of one day, in Methodist Hospital. I took him home that one day, only to have to take him back. Everyone thought he wasn't going to make it, but it was not God's time for him.

He was on Main 8, North West. I want to give those wonderful nurses the credit and thanks they deserve. I especially want to thank one nurse, Betty Brown, who was so kind and comforting to me. I just talked to her this week and asked if I could use her name. She reminded me that I used to sing to Duane. I did that much of his life.

I stayed with Duane all the time while he was in Methodist. There were a lot of very hard times for both of us. Once they were taking him off to a room for a surgical procedure. All at once, I ran to the desk to remind them he was a Do Not Resuscitate.

Can you imagine what that was like for me? I was saying, "If his heart stops, don't start it again." Having to write this is so painful, but those were his wishes. We had the signed papers. It was all legal, but, oh, how that hurts to say. My heart goes out to all of you who either have experienced this or are about to do so. God is our strength. Even if you do not have a relationship with Him, He loves you and will hear your cry to Him.

You can imagine that over a period of a month, Duane and I would find things that would bring about laughter. Once I went to the gift shop for snacks and stuff, and came back with a stuffed Tweety Bird. He loved it.

A week or so later, I got him Snoopy, topped with a cowboy hat. He wanted to see what else I had in my bag. He kept on until I had to admit that in the rush to get to the hospital, I had forgotten to pack extra panties. We just laughed and laughed. I know, he was my grown son, but when you think someone is dying, you let your guard down and get very real.

You do know, don't you, that laughter relieves tension, exercises your insides, and delays ugly wrinkles? Those around your eyes and smile lines are beautiful.

On another day they were doing a surgical procedure in his room to remove Duane's central line in his left shoulder, and insert a Hickman in the right shoulder. They thought the central line was infected, so they were removing it. I made phone calls down the hall, while the staff worked on Duane. I returned not realizing they hadn't finished so I waited outside his room. He was always so brave, but all at once I heard Duane make a deep, painful wail. I nearly came out of my skin!

I first thought how Daddy had told me to "be his brave little girl" when I was going to the operating room for my appendectomy.

I thought, "God, help me be brave. Help Duane be brave." Then I thought, "I don't want to be the Mother. I want to be the little girl." Later the nurse said what a rough surgery it was.

We were both so glad that was over. I don't remember when they put in another line. We were grateful for the fact that this was how he got his nutrition.

They were still battling high fevers. Finally the doctor decided to try a "Cold Blanket." They look rather like the egg shaped toppers used on mattresses. The difference is a Cold Blanket has ice water running through it. Duane was lying on that for hours. One night, he was so miserably cold that he asked, "Mother, may I come lie on your cot with you?" I said, "Sure Honey. I helped him lie down by me.

As we lay there together, he said, "Mother, I am so tired. Why doesn't my body just shut down?" I responded, very lovingly, "Honey, you inherited a strong heart from my daddy and you have a strong spirit. Those two things are hard to beat."

Then I prayed silently to God, "Please, Father, release my baby from his body. Let him come home and be with you."

A year later Duane and I talked about that hospital stay. I said, "You wanted to have it all end. I actually asked God to take you. Aren't you glad I don't have that much influence on God? We have had another whole year." Again, we had a good laugh.

As I said, there were things we saw as amusing. There was one night nurse who was so sweet, but clumsy. One night she stepped on Duane's line, which scared us both. Remember, that hurts a lot when it goes in or out. I'm sure she never realized she had done that. When I would see her coming, I would say, "Oops, here comes the clumsy ox. I've got your line in my hand, so she can't step on it." We had many laughs over her, but she never knew it. We would never have hurt her feelings; I just protected him.

As many of you know, when you are in the hospital, often you don't see your regular doctor. A hospital doctor is assigned to you. As a rule, I am very easy to get along with, but if you give my ill family member a difficult time, then the gloves go on and I come out swinging.

Duane had been on the Cold Blanket and his temp finally came down. The doctor was going to send him home immediately. I said, "No, I am not taking him home until we see if his temp is going to stay down."

Well, he was rather insistent, so I said, "Okay, then you get me a machine (it was about the size of a washer) like this to have if he starts running a fever again." I suppose he didn't want to argue, so he said, "Well, I don't think they are available." I said that maybe we could rent one. I was desperate!

After awhile the doctor called back and said, "I don't think those machines can be rented." I said, "Well, don't you say one thing to anyone and ruin my chances of success. I have trained salespeople for years, and I guarantee you that if you don't think you can help me, you can't! And, we are not going home today. Let me tell you something, we are not going to resuscitate him, but we are not going to fry his brain either!"

The next morning, the doctor came by to see Duane before I awoke. He said, "I think I owe your mother an apology. I was not very helpful. I had just read a bad report on Cold Blankets."

When I woke up and Duane told me what the doctor had said, we both laughed and he said, "I guess he won't mess with you anymore. I really do appreciate you, Mother. I know you will always take care of me." You may have figured out by now that I am a formidable foe or advocate, whichever is called for, when it comes to my family.

We finally did get to take Duane home on July 27th. They had called in a specialist, who ran tests and found that he was short on Vitamin K. There may have been other things too, but I remember being so grateful that they discovered that deficiency.

Once again, I want to thank Methodist Hospital, Main 8, NW for the marvelous care, consideration, and comfort they gave Duane and me.

From my notes, I gather I stayed in Houston for a couple of weeks after he left the hospital. During that summer Dudley and I found out we couldn't be away from each other more than a week or ten days. Then he would fly to Houston to see both me and Duane.

I wrote the following in my journal: "Dudley and I have known each other as friends even before we had our children. Now we are getting to know each other as husband and wife. No one could have seen this in the long ago…only God."

Once while speaking with Stephanie during that long summer, she said, "We want you to come home. We miss you!" What a great God we have. How wonderful it was that He gave me my new family before He took my son!

I was back in Houston in August. Duane was very weak and anemic. A nurse came to his apartment and gave him several units of blood. It was a long day. Before he received the transfusions, he could barely get to the bathroom next door. After receiving the blood and a good night's rest, I observed a miracle.

When I got up at 6:00 a.m. the next morning, and saw he was not in his bed, I was frightened. I found him at his computer, working away. He turned and gave me that big, beautiful smile of his and said, "Good morning, Mother."

I learned something at a deep level that day about my faith. All Christians know that Jesus died on the cross as payment for our sins. We hear about His shedding of the blood. We even used to sing a song, *There is Power in the Blood*. I don't think I ever really understood about this "blood thing." Finally, I saw a living example of the fact that "the life is in the blood." Duane had no energy, then he got the blood, then he had energy! Truly, there is power in the blood.

At this stage in Duane's disease, we were always adjusting his medications. I had a list of meds I carried at all times, along with a large blue binder with his legal papers filed in it, with phone numbers of doctors and friends in Houston and Dallas. It was very helpful.

When Duane called and said, "I'm going to the hospital, get here as quickly as you can," I was always ready. This happened a lot that last year or so. It is amazing what we can do when we have to do it!

My new family could not have been more wonderful to me. Stephanie and I were growing closer all the time. She loved the fact that I was such a goofy grandmother. Sarah was a really good baby. She was happy and so much fun. Duane loved to hear her in the background when he called. He was so very happy for me, because he knew I loved my new life.

In August, Duane called and left a message, "Please call my doctor. I'm in pain. I need a higher dose of pain killer. I have coughed all day. I haven't kept food down. I'm okay; not dying; just hurting." Of course, I contacted his doctor and she ordered more medication.

As I write, I realize that I cry out to God, just like Duane would cry out to me for help. I was and am still his mother. God is my Father and He hears my cries and responds to me with even a greater love than I had for Duane. If you get nothing from this book, I pray you experience God's love in a new, even more wonderful way than you ever have before. He is there for you. He is not against you. Even when He says "no" it is for our good, even when we can't understand it.

Dudley and I were ecstatically happy. We both loved being in love and having someone love us totally and completely in spite of our faults. Really, we didn't see each other's faults. As I told a young couples Sunday school class, "In spite of what you think (everyone loved Dud), Dudley was not a perfect man, and I am certainly not a perfect woman, but we had an almost perfect marriage." What a gift at this time in our lives!

Sometime that fall, we learned that Duane's roommate was going to be moving. Duane could not afford to live there alone, so he started looking for a smaller apartment. He found one that was perfect for him, near the end of the building, just six steps to the parking lot. There were windows which gave him lots of light and he was able to keep most of his furniture. He kept his oriental rug for his living room, which is now in my home.

Duane didn't have enough income to qualify for the apartment, so my wonderful husband and his Dad (Dud), put the apartment in his name. Dudley and I were both on the phone one day. Someone at the leasing office was giving him a hard time. Dudley asked, "Do you want me to come down and kick _____?" (You fill in the blank. He was a preacher, but also a Dad.) Duane responded, "Don't think I didn't think about sickin' you on them."

As Duane said, "When Dad calls me 'son' I just melt." He finally had a real Daddy who knew how to love him!

In early November, Duane called, saying he was hurting all over. His arms weren't strong enough to pick up a pitcher. He had neuropathy in his hands now. He was getting 1.6 mil. of pain medication every two hours. Even in the hospital they only gave 2 mil., unless you were terminal.

"I can barely hold the phone, it's like rigor mortis has set in," he explained; "Maybe I died and no one told me, or maybe I died and I am too stubborn to lie down." This was one of the few times I heard real discouragement in his voice and words.

A friend of Duane's worked for the Houston Grand Opera. They had held an auction as a fund raiser, where two tickets for a cruise to the Greek Islands were offered. Dud and I were able to get them at a good price.

Dudley said, "Well, while we are that close, let's just go on to the Holy Land." It took me all of half of a second to say, "Oh, that would be wonderful! I have always wanted to go to Jerusalem, but never thought I would get to go." Planning the trip gave Duane something to do for his new Dad. We had a wonderful time thanks to Duane's loving effort.

Even though there were some tough times, Duane kept pursuing life. One day he told me that he had been to a renaissance festival and had a great time.

He was getting excited about his new apartment. Of course, there wasn't much he could do to prepare for the move. Some of his friends helped with the packing, and of course, "You-Know-Who" did most of it. I am so grateful that I was still young and healthy enough to do this for him.

There was a large deposit at stake when Duane moved out. There had been several guys moving in and out over the years, and lots of "stuff" was abandoned in the attic.

Duane's friend, Libby came to help me get it down. There were things too big for either of us to carry down the ladder.

Get ready to chuckle! Our Bible stories came in handy. Do you remember the men letting down the man from the roof for healing? Well, we took a board and tied ropes around each end and lowered the big stuff on that board. When we have to, women can get creative. We didn't get anyone healed, but we certainly got that apartment empty and as clean as a whistle. Every penny counted, and we got the entire deposit back, which really helped Duane.

Duane's friend, Larry, helped with the new apartment, by exterminating the rooms, and washing down the cabinets. We moved Duane on November 22, 1997. It was a one year lease. Duane said, "That is probably all I will need." He was right.

No matter what we were doing, we always had lots of fun. Duane was a master at hanging pictures. He had a great eye for that. He took his trusty little hammer and hung to his heart's delight as he said, "I am putting everything I want up on the wall. When I am gone, it will be your job to get your deposit back!" We both laughed like two little kids doing something naughty. I sure do miss him!

I hope you are getting a picture of what a special person he was. Even though there was a lot of pain involved for him, we were both so thankful we had those last couple of years.

CHAPTER 10
Music to My Ears

* * *

Dudley and I began Thanksgiving Day by faxing our Houston son the following message: Good morning Son! Dad and I want to wish you a Happy Thanksgiving. I am so very grateful, Duane, for our "Special Times" this past year. You are the most wonderful son a mother could ever have. Thanks for being you and for loving me. We Love You, Mother & Dad.

Our Dancer Thanksgiving was wonderful. Then to top it off, I received a very special call from Duane. He had a great day and wanted to share his experience with me. As he had written in one of the books he gave me for Mother's Day, we loved talking nearly every day. You might say that by now our relationship was nearly flawless. It was like it was when he was younger, except even better because now we were adult to adult. That is, until those moments when he wanted to be my baby. I did love that kid. I say "kid" out of love. I so respected the wonderful man he had become.

Duane was anxious to tell me about his day. He had gone to church for a service and a meal. His day was filled with gratitude for all that God had done for him and given to him. After filling me in on the day's activities he related the following conversation.

One of his male friends came up and said, "Oh, Duane, I met the cutest guy, but (and his voice changes) he is a (snarling) Christian."

Duane replied, "Now wait a minute. We don't want to be judged by the Christians, so we shouldn't judge them. Besides, my mother is a Christian. I have wanted her to approve my lifestyle all my life. I now understand that she will never approve my lifestyle, because according to her faith, it is a sin. But, I have the best mother in the world. She is here for me physically, emotionally, or spiritually anytime I need her or even want her."

You can just imagine how fantastic it felt to me to hear Duane talk about me in those terms to a gay friend. You see, all those years of standing firm on my beliefs, but in unconditional love certainly did pay off. So many people think you can't give this kind of supportive, nurturing, caring love when you can't affirm a person's behavior.

As far as I see it, this is the kind of love God gives us if we allow it. I know God has always loved me, but I know there have been times He could not affirm my behavior. When I went to Him in true repentance and asked for forgiveness, I was forgiven. Have I repeated that same sin? Yes, but not so often. With God's help my resistance has grown stronger.

Because of God's unconditional love towards me, I have been able to let that same love flow through me, not only to Duane, but to others as well. Don't misunderstand me, I can't always achieve that, but God and I are working on me all the time.

This event and Duane's call showed me that God was revealing Himself more and more to Duane. That was exciting to me, but I always tried to keep my joy low-keyed. I didn't want to mess up what God was doing in and for Duane.

Thanksgiving was a hint of things to come. It was the start of something great and God allowed me to have a front row seat to what He was doing in both our lives.

December was a month of resettling after the move. I went to Houston once or twice to help, and Duane had a precious cleaning lady, Beverly. She moved unpacked boxes into the closet to give us more room, and unpacked several boxes herself. Duane said, "Beverly is one of my heroes."

Juan hung some of the pictures that Duane couldn't manage. With an illness like his, it takes a lot of help. Thank God, he had wonderful friends. Juan had made the decision to stay in Houston. Duane was very humbled and grateful.

Back in Dallas, we were hustling around getting ready for a very special Christmas. This was Sarah's first. Even Santa was more excited than usual. As I have told you before, Dudley and I were so "into" being grandparents. This was a special joy that I had never shared with anyone else, but Dudley. You can probably sense that I simply adored my sweet husband!

Soon after Christmas, Dudley, Mike, and I went to Houston to celebrate with Duane. We had a great time. I specifically remember the three of them on the couch singing, *Oh, Lord, it's hard to be humble*. They were so funny and surprisingly they actually sounded pretty good.

Dudley and Mike returned to Dallas, but I stayed over to be with Duane for New Year's Day. We went to Duane's church while I was there. It was a beautiful Sunday morning. His pastor talked about how the human race had pulled themselves up from little amoebas. He mentioned how wonderful Sister Teresa was and that she was an example of how far one can grow by her own efforts.

For lunch we were seated in a cozy booth, so Duane and I were eye to eye. We chatted a bit then he asked, "What did you think of my preacher?" Without hesitating I responded, "I think he is a very nice man, but I feel sort of sorry for him."

When he asked why, I continued, "Well, I believe I was created by God and that makes me feel special. I was actually raised with the attitude of pulling ourselves up by our own bootstraps. Those of us who were lucky, had our bootstraps break somewhere along the way and we discovered Someone else had been holding us up all along."

Duane said, "Hey, Mom that is good. That is deep, really deep." I replied with a simple "thanks." I didn't make a big deal over it, but again, I could see God was working on his mind. I don't think his heart was ever the issue. It was his mind and what was he to do with his homosexual desires? That was what created the complexity of his life.

Life is never easy or simple. I heard Dr. Joe Neely, a Bible teacher at Lovers Lane United Methodist in Dallas say something recently. He was speaking of the laws and rules of God. He said, "God's rules show what God values." I love that. I have always said that God didn't tell us not to do this or that to mess up our fun, but if we follow His rules, life goes well and we can be happy. I like the simplicity of what Joe said.

By this stage in Duane's life, I was usually in Houston every two or three weeks. Sometime in January 1998, I went to see Duane. One day he said, without any fanfare or warning, "I know what I am." I wondered what I was about to hear, because he said this with such conviction. Very quietly I said, "Oh."

He went on to tell me, "I am a Christian. I believe Jesus is the Son of God. I believe He is the only man who ever lived without sinning. I believe in His sacrifice on the cross for my sins. I had a "real" experience with Jesus as a boy at First Baptist, Richardson."

In my mind, I am going chink, chink, chink. I think that is it. More than anything, the part about Jesus' sacrifice on the cross for his sins was the statement that really nailed it for me. That wasn't Duane lingo. That was a real conviction statement.

I had waited so long to hear these words. There was a part of me that was almost afraid to breathe for fear I would mess up the moment. This was quite a declaration! God had shown me back in 1991 that this would happen, but it had been so long that sometimes I thought maybe I had misunderstood. These were the words I longed to hear. Now I could be at peace about him dying, even though I wanted to have some more sweet times with him.

So what great answer did I give to this wonderful spiritual declaration my son had made? If I remember right, it was something so profound as, "I am so happy for you, son."

I was calm on the outside, but I was jumping up and down and shouting on the inside! At last, at last, my baby had returned to his sweet relationship with Jesus.

There was more good news to come. However, before we get to that, there were more difficult days for Duane, physically. I don't remember why I took him to Methodist Hospital, but he had an X-ray and CAT scan done on January 31st.

On February 6th, I took him to see a different doctor. I can't remember what her specialty was, but it evidently was connected with the CAT scan.

He sat in a chair, while she stood directly in front of him. I was sitting over to the side. As he looked up at her, she reached over and touching the left side of his forehead, she said, "On the film there is a cold spot right here, which could be a tumor." She had barely finished her sentence when he said, "Oh, that's where the aliens invaded my body!"

Truthfully, I don't remember what she said after he and I stopped laughing. In all actuality, it probably was no laughing matter, but after awhile when you deal with any kind of a horrible disease, you either develop a weird sense of humor or you cry all the time. It was never our style to cry all the time. Yes, we had our moments, I have shared many with you, but they weren't all the time.

As I think back about all this, we both cried more over our broken relationship than we did about any health problems either of us had. I understand that not everyone sees humor in life's problems, but to me, it makes endurance easier. We didn't plan on it, or work at it, humor was a gift from God.

Some time during the first part of the year, Duane had a fungus develop in his throat. As a result of it, he could only whisper. We still called each other, but didn't talk as long. That may be why we did the CAT scan.

I faxed a note to him on February 25th, which happened to be Ash Wednesday. It read: Dad just called to tell me about your call to him. He doesn't cry easily, but tears were there. He said, "I was concerned about our services, one at noon and the other in the evening. Now I know they are going to be fine." Our precious son, you have given Dad the most wonderful gift of the Lenten season. Dad said, "He touched me so. I will never forget this call." You are a magnificent man. We are so blessed to be your parents. Thanks Duane, for all you are. Have a wonderful day. See you tomorrow. I Love You Very Much! Mother.

I have no idea what the conversation was about. I am sure Dudley told me at the time, or maybe not. He was a person who knew how to keep confidences. Sometimes he would say someone I knew had come by to see him. We never talked about why. I never asked. We really were a perfect match! Duane and he are now sharing their great love for each other in Heaven. I am glad they have each other.

Around the middle of March, Duane was running fever and then chills. His gums were bleeding. His platelet count was high. They wanted him to go to the hospital, but he refused.

It must have been about this time, he burned himself, but I can't remember the incident. He must have gone to the hospital without me, which was unusual. I had notes from April 7th saying his doctor didn't think the fever and chills were from the burn. They were playing with meds, trying to give him some relief from pain.

I e-mailed Juan and asked about the burn. Here is the story:

> *"I clearly remember that it was a week day (probably Thursday) around 7 p.m. when I got a call from Duane saying that he had an accident at his kitchen with burning oil which produced burnings on his chest and stomach areas. I ran immediately to his home and got there at the same time that the ambulance and paramedics did. They rushed him to the hospital while I was driving behind them in my car. Duane was hungry and had a taste for a pork chop, he started cooking pouring lots of oil in a pan, once when it was very hot he dropped with a little too much 'energy' the pork chop at the pan and oil got spilled on his chest. As you remember he loved to be with no shirt at home so...he was unprotected. We spent the night at the hospital; he was released the following day. I was not sure what bothered him most...being burned by oil or not being able to enjoy his pork chop...hehehehehe... Fortunately he had a quick recovery.*

I love the way Juan told the story. It made me chuckle about Duane not being able to enjoy his pork chop. As I read this, I thought, "Those last couple of years, Juan was on the front line. Then when needed or desired, they called in the 'big guns'. Of course, that was me! Duane had some kind of surgical procedure done on the 17th, and I was there, because I signed the discharge papers. I also found the following note:

"Oh God, I need You! I hurt! Four hours alone while waiting. My mind goes crazy. I start thinking what will I do if they come out and say Duane is gone? My eyes fill–in my mind–I scream and cry–I go to my baby–I hold him and talk to You."

It is strange that I don't remember this. You can feel the agony I was feeling. I am surprised I didn't call some of his friends. Yet, I am not surprised. I have dealt with so many, many extremely hard things all alone. No, not alone. I have always had my Lord and Savior, my Father God, and my loving, kind, Holy Spirit! Christianity is not just a ticket to Heaven. It is a fabulous relationship with Almighty God right now! He will never leave you, nor forsake you.

Because of all these hospital trips and things going wrong, you can see why I needed to get the papers signed to authorize cremation. Even though I was Duane's legal medical power of attorney, I had to get his father to sign the papers too.

We were about to take our wonderful cruise to the Greek Islands and tour of the Holy Land which Duane so skillfully helped us plan. We were leaving on April 22nd and returning on May 11th. Considering Duane's health, being gone seemed pretty scary. Thankfully our very capable and willing son, Mike, assured us he would be the medical contact in case of an emergency. There are not enough words in the English language to tell you what a great son he was to his dad and then to me after I married his dad. He has brought me a great deal of joy.

I left Mike and our daughter, Stephanie, a complete itinerary with a detailed list of phone numbers, including friends, doctors, relatives, our church, Duane's church, and yes, even the funeral home. Thank God, the kids didn't need any of those numbers.

Dudley and I had an absolutely glorious time. We even did okay with our tiny ship bathroom. That was probably because Dud was very patient with me. He would go get me breakfast while I got ready for the day.

We had an outside cabin so we could look out, which we both loved. We had two twin beds and we were not about to sleep that way, so we pushed them together. After all, we were newlyweds.

We loved the Greek islands and our trip to the Holy Land was fabulous. One of our favorite experiences was having

Communion on a bench right beside the Garden of Gethsemane. We had a free day at the end of our tour. At breakfast, we got the idea for our venture to Gethsemane. We had loaves of bread and water. I said, "Jesus turned water into wine. I think you can ask Jesus to bless our water and use it for Communion." Poor Dudley, he never knew what to expect from me; neither did I (ha, ha). He loved my spontaneity. Our time together was not as long as we had hoped it would be, but it was a glorious time!

We loved the Sea of Galilee and both had a deep spiritual experience at the Garden Tomb. I won't take your time telling you all about our trip, but if you get to that part of the world, check out Ephesus.

Once home, it was back to the reality of our lives with our family. Some of you have heard me say that in the Christian life there are periods where we just don't seem to see God working in our lives. I confess that occasionally I have looked up towards Heaven and waved my arm and said, "Hey, God, it's me, Elaine, did You forget me down here?" Now really, I have always known that I have never been off His mind; it has just felt that way.

On the other hand, when you see that God is beginning to move in your life, it is a good idea to hang on, because often times it is almost like dominoes being knocked down. Again, chink, chink, chink. That is what I saw in Duane's life.

One day, as we spoke on the phone he told me that Juan was into Hare Krishna and liked to look at a picture of him as he prayed. He wanted to warn me that he had a picture of Krishna on the wall of the living room. Then he said, "For equal time, if you would like to bring a picture of Jesus, that would be good." Then he went on to ask me not to bring a picture of Jesus on the cross. I was thrilled and assured him I would find one I was sure he would like.

Duane was a fantastic man in so many ways. One of his greatest qualities was that he didn't see anyone as being better than anyone else. He never saw "color". People were just people to him. They weren't black or white or Indian or Chinese. They were all worthy of our kindness and respect. It is truly a shame he could not have lived longer. He was a wonderful person and yes, I might be a little prejudiced, but most people would agree with me.

Duane also loved little children. So I found the perfect picture of Jesus to take to him. In the picture, Jesus is surrounded by little children of all different colors. Duane loved it and I was so happy to give it to him. I thought, "I don't think Jesus would mind Krishna on the wall, if that is what it took to get His picture on the wall too." By the way, I thought Krishna was going to be some older, bearded man. In the picture at Duane's home, he was a baby, rather cherub looking. It didn't give me the "willies" after all.

I could see God really working in Duane's life. A few weeks later, he told me I could bring him a Bible. I really don't know if he read it or not, but at least he asked for it and I took it.

One of the things I miss most about Duane is that even though he loved me dearly, he could be very objective about my situations. He could sort of stand off to the side and look at things as they really are, not always how he would like to see them. Our only big issue was the homosexual lifestyle. By this time, he had accepted I would never be able to affirm the lifestyle, but always be there for him with my unconditional love and support.

Because of his whisper, we faxed some, but still had sweet short phone calls. He tried to get me interested in e-mail. I balked, for which I am very sorry. We could have enjoyed that form of conversation.

We talked on May 19th, and he was feeling better. He had been to church and a movie. He told me of a new experience he recently had. A church friend had committed suicide in

December. They had buried the ashes and covered them with leaves from a retreat. He was one of six people at the service. He enjoyed the intimacy and respect. It was a tender, comforting ceremony. I'm certain it made his own death seem extremely real. However, he didn't feel death was eminent.

I faxed him a Happy 35th Birthday greeting and spoke with him briefly. We had sent him a Coca Cola ceiling fan which he loved.

I went down on the 26th and spent four and a half days with him. One day, as we were getting ready to go somewhere, he was shaving, and I was in the hallway near him. We had disco music going and I was putting on my earrings.

He said, "You know Mother, when you tell everyone you are coming to see me, they think you are sitting by my bed with me going 'Awww'. They have no idea how much fun we have!" We both had a good laugh.

Another time he said, "I suppose if I could snap my fingers and not have AIDS, I would do it. I'm not sure though. If I were well, I would be over at Foley's in a meeting, arguing for ad money, instead of being here having fun with my Mother." One does get a sense of what is important at times like these.

By this time, Dudley and I were so enjoying doing ministry together. I was speaking a couple of times a month to different classes at the church and sometimes assisting Dud with his Sunday evening worship service. I loved praying beside him at the altar at the end of the service. Then to close we would all form a large circle around the sanctuary. As we held hands, we would sing "Alleluia". I loved looking at the faces, as we sang. It was an opportunity to connect with people and get to know them. Those were great days!

Oh, I just thought of something rather funny and sweet. I have already told you how Dudley and Duane's love for each other just grew and grew. Dud started calling him "Duanie Boy". Now, no one else could ever have gotten by with that. It was a pet name Dud gave him. I never called him that, but now occasionally I pick up a picture of him and Dud and say, "I love you, Duanie Boy and Dud." Well, yes, I just shed a tear.

While in Houston the last of June, Duane told me about leaving the post office one day when a man in his 30ies or 40ies approached him. He admitted that he looked rather scruffy. The man said, "Are you in need of prayer for healing?" Duane answered, "Yes, please." Then the man said, "Have you found God?" And he continued, "I will pray for you now!" And he did! He seemed very sincere when he said, "I am a minister. I will be praying for you; expect a healing."

After telling me about this encounter, he said, "I am jealous of that kind of faith." He was getting closer to being totally healed, but it was going to be on the other side, in the presence of Jesus.

Duane had so many people who had prayed for him for such a long time. JoAnne, one of my sweet friends from the Ardmore area would say, "Father, deal with Duane, but gently." Another friend, Dee Hutson, kept Duane's and my names and faces before the Lord and our friends for years. On July 25th my sister Evelyn said, "Just last night I was praying and said, "You must not be ready to take him. When you do, take him peacefully."

By this time, Stephanie, Sarah, and I spent a lot of time together. As I have said before, we loved to go shopping. We have laughed so many times, as we think about one of the first things Sarah ever said was, "Let's go shopping!" Even when she was young, she would walk up to a rack and with her little index finger she would flip through the hangers just like we all do. Steph and I would laugh and laugh.

Duane was so happy that I had my adorable little granddaughter. He gave her a Llama and a book entitled, "Llama in pajamas." We have a picture of her when she was perhaps four months old holding the book as though she were "reading" it. He would say, "Now when she is Valedictorian of her class, you tell her that Uncle Duane gave her the first book she ever read."

Once that summer, Duane and I were headed toward the parking lot at his apartment, when he said, "See that tall building over there? I spent a weekend on an elevator there." He went on to say that he was drugged up and was crumpled in a corner of the elevator. He said, "People came and went, and I went up and down, up and down."

When I said, "Oh, Honey," he said, "It is okay now Mother. Just look at us and how much fun we are having." I am so grateful that he trusted me enough to tell me even those things which I didn't want to hear.

This story reminds me of how God can turn things around for us. Do you remember how sick I was on the farm, and had to return to Dallas with virtually nothing? Well, I would often say, "God is going to restore the years of the locust."

One day in Houston, Duane and I had gone to the grocery store. His feet were bad, so he waited at the entrance while I got the car. When he got into the car he smiled and said, "Mother, when you would say, "God was going to restore the years of the locust, I would think, at her age, how is He going to do that?" Just now, as I watched you walking to your Cadillac, I thought, "She was right. God has restored the years of the locust." We had a big laugh together as I said, "That's true, God has." I am so blessed to have all these wonderful memories! Whatever you do, don't shut your loved ones out.

Duane was in a specialty hospital for three days in August, for adjustments to his TPN (nutrition). They were also administering a type of chemo they referred to as "shake and bake."

A few days after he got home, he was going to see his friend, Carol. He was so happy, since he hadn't seen her for two or three months. It might have been because she had a new baby girl. He had such good friends. People loved being with him, because he made them feel so special.

As nice as he was, Duane could be pushed too far. On August 18th, he had been to a speech therapist. He could still only whisper. This had been going on for nearly a year. She had advised, "Just talk softly." He told me, "I wanted to hit her!" You see, he couldn't talk; he had no voice because of the fungus.

He and another lady, Barbara, from his church had run errands one day. He said he felt embarrassed by his body. I remembered thinking how badly one of my friends had looked, and God had said, "Elaine, he is not his body." That is so freeing for all of us.

As one of my preacher friends who is about my age said recently, "Have you looked in the mirror lately?" Our bodies change over a course of a lifetime. Sometimes we can do something about it, sometimes we can't. Acceptance is a remarkable quality.

Duane went on that day, telling me different thoughts he had. He said, "I have been sexually impotent for three years. I don't even think sexually."

It was in August that the radio program, Focus On The Family, held a conference called "Renewing the Heart" in San Antonio. Dear, sweet Dudley, paid all the expenses for me, Stephanie, our neighbor, Marilyn, and his secretary, Suzanne to go. We had a glorious time. They had sent us a cassette tape of the worship music we would be singing. We all just loved the music.

When I told Duane I was going he said, "Oh, Mother, I am so happy for you. Go and laugh and talk with the girls, and Be Filled With The Spirit!" I thought, "Wow, that is not Duane's kind of language. That is the Holy Spirit speaking." This was another piece of the puzzle.

CHAPTER 11

On with His Spiritual Journey

* * *

The next thing I saw in Duane as he skipped down this spiritual journey was something he said to me on August 28th. Stephanie and her husband, Zenon opened a restaurant with Dudley's help, and we were all excited about it.

On that Friday night, they were all at the restaurant. The place was packed; everyone was having a great time. Duane called and I said, "I have always been the mover and shaker. They are all having a great time and I am home caring for Sarah." (Yes, a bit of a pity party, I admit it.)

Duane's response was quick. He said, "Oh, Mother, you are doing the most important job of all. You are building into Sarah, her inner core. In spite of how screwed up I was, I made my spiritual recovery because of what you taught me, and your love for me and your love for Jesus!" He went on to talk about how entire families have no inner core and how grateful he was for me.

Wow, no more pity party for me. What music to my ears! Holding strong to my beliefs, but doing so in love, had paid off Big Time! Thank You, Jesus.

September 9th was Juan's birthday. When I spoke to Duane, he was very sick. He said, "I am lower than a worm underneath a rock. The good news is that I am now getting housekeeping two times a week." What a guy, no matter how sick he was he most always could find something to be happy about. I was so proud of him.

Our restaurant chef was excellent, and Dudley had the idea of taking a meal down to Duane and Juan. Of course, they loved the idea, too! So we began to put the plan together. We faxed the menu. They selected what they wanted.

Then our boy called and asked, "Could Jon and Stephanie (Duane's Houston friends) come too?" Jon was Duane's old roommate. He and Stephanie had just gotten married. We said, of course, they could come and we got their selections from the menu. Stephanie was in an opera, so couldn't come on our first choice of nights. That was no problem. We changed the date to September 25th, which was a Friday night. We were taking everything we needed, including a beautiful linen tablecloth I purchased when Duane and I went to Europe.

Before we could have this fabulous dinner party, Duane needed some new clothes. I went down and we shopped for an entire day. It was quite a challenge. He had lost so much weight, that all the men's clothes just swallowed him. Finally, someone told us about a children's specialty shop. They were so nice to us. We bought him a suit, a blue blazer, slacks, and some shirts. Oh, yes, and some new ties. He was a business man, and like his mother, he liked to look the part. He was very tired, but happy, by the end of the day.

We were all set for the 25th! Little did we know this would be his last dinner party. Dudley and I were both a little prone to procrastinating, so the fact that we did not do so with this event is some kind of a miracle.

Duane was having trouble with his sinus passages. I took him to a doctor who said that cleaning them out might not do his nose or his throat any good. I was a little hesitant to go forward, but it was not my decision. Duane wanted to talk again so badly, and I can certainly relate to that. For those of us who are relationship people, talking is who we are.

The doctor performed the procedure on the 25th; that's right, the day of our dinner party. When we arrived two hours or so before our scheduled time, Duane was sitting in the middle of his bed, with a pan of blood in front of him. He was trying to get the bleeding stopped. When we walked in the front door to his apartment, we could see straight into his room. Even in that situation, he flashed one of those heart stopping smiles and his eyes lit up as he said, "Hi! Welcome! I'm so excited!"

I took one look at him and asked, "Are you going to be up to coming to the table in two hours?" He responded quickly, "Sure. I will be fine by then! I have a little, bitty voice, but it is my voice." He was so happy, that it was heart wrenching. How I loved him. He was one of the bravest men I have ever known.

Juan, Jon, and Stephanie arrived a few minutes before 7:00 p.m. Duane had taken a shower, put on his suit and appeared as though nothing difficult had happened earlier.

Duane and his guests enjoyed the food, while Dudley and I served, white aprons and all. We even made a video that night. We told funny stories, as we laughed and laughed. The only sad moment was when Jon and Stephanie announced to Duane they were leaving town. I already knew, but hadn't told Duane. They wanted to share the news themselves. Duane was sad for himself, but happy for them, as Jon was going to a better job. Besides, after his moment of sadness, Duane turned over his tie so Jon could see the label, "Look, it is from the Metropolitan Museum of Arts." We lingered over the table, reminiscing, remembering the past, and talking about our futures. It was a great night! As I sometimes say, "A real God deal!"

Dudley had to return to Dallas the next day for Sunday services, but I stayed over. Before Dudley left, we celebrated my birthday! Juan was so dear. He had gotten one of those candles that play "Happy Birthday". Duane gave me a beautiful Hummel porcelain tea set, with the "Stormy Weather" print on it. He knew I loved the Hummel figurines I had. Oh, he did know his mother and I knew him.

The next day Juan stayed with Duane while I went shopping for some soft new towels for him. He had always loved soaking in the tub. Now, a bath was especially soothing to his little wasted body.

We saw the nose and throat doctor on Monday. I realized all his doctors were getting pretty tense, but I didn't know what they all suspected.

Tuesday, we had another marvelously fun day. We bought books at Borders for Duane and books for me to give as Christmas presents. On the receipt, which I still have, I wrote, "with Duane...a fun day." We also went to a special men's shirt store and got shirts for Dudley and ties for both Duane and Dud.

We had lunch somewhere, maybe Mexican. This makes me think of a time, perhaps the year before when we were looking at a menu and I didn't know how to pronounce a word or what it meant. He made some remark which sort of hurt my feelings. He picked up on it, and with tears in his eyes, said how sorry he was. He was always sweet, but in those last couple of years, he became the most tender-hearted person I have ever known.

I wish I had done a better job of journaling but I am grateful that I took notes when we talked on the phone. On Wednesday, Sept. 30th, I wrote: "My darling Son, I feel so close to you today. It is going to be hard to leave you. I probably won't be back for a month. We have had such a wonderful visit—our Bistro dinner—our Border's book store finds—our new Jewish men friends where we bought shirts (two for you—one and a tie for Juan's birthday)—our trip to Dr. Jimenez and Debra's (the nurse practitioner) visit. Our trip back to the book store and bought you ties—our making of the videos—one for Dottie and one for Stephanie and Zenon. We also saw "One Real Thing"—the story of a woman dying with cancer and her relationship to her family. It was hard for both of us to watch her suffer your kind of pain—physical and emotional—but we drew closer watching it. I went to sleep twice this visit lying on your shoulder. I do love you so much. Thanks for the memories!"

This was also the day Duane was sitting at his computer and told me, "I want you to go educate the world." As I have said before, Big Job!

Duane at His Computer

I did return to Dallas that day. I always drove. I liked having my car while there, and actually love car trips. I turn on Christian music, or some other kind, or listen to tapes of my preacher friends, or turn everything off and just spend quality time with God. I drove to Houston so many times that I could just get into my car and say "Houston", and off we went. I had all my stopping points, which weren't many. Once I get into the car, it is pretty much...go!

CHAPTER 12
The Final Days

* * *

I was always going to Houston for a fun time with my son, or going because he was in trouble and needed his mother. Either way, I was so grateful that Dudley made it possible for me to quit my job and concentrate on my family, both in Dallas and Houston.

On Thursday night, Duane hit his face with a tray. It caused a deviated septum. He had lots of pain and was blowing puss from his nose. He heated a mask and placed it on his face, which helped some. Juan bought a steam inhaler for him. By Saturday night, it was a little better. However, he was still bleeding from his sinus. He did feel good enough on Saturday to go to the Yoga Center, which Juan ran.

When we spoke on Monday, he was having chills, and then his fever would go up to 102. Tylenol would bring it down temporarily.

Tuesday night was a wonderful evening for Dudley and me. Dud is such a blessing to our entire family. When we got home, I got the message from Duane. He had called about 6:00 p.m. saying to call as soon as possible. By the time I called, his fever had gone down.

I sat down and wrote the following:

My teeth are clinched. My stomach is in a knot. I can't think. There is much to do, but I think I will go to bed. It is 12:35 a.m. Duane is running high fevers again. This morning it was almost 104. Tonight it was 104.2. I want to scream! I want to cry! God, how does my darling son keep fighting this horrible disease AIDS? I talked to him about 10:00 p.m. Finally, as I write this, the tears begin to flow. Oh, Father God, how I love You! I would surely go crazy without You! My Baby! My Baby! How long must he suffer? I don't want to lose him, but I can hardly stand to see him go on like this.

Now, Father, I don't know if I will go to Oklahoma to see my family as planned. I don't feel very comfortable being that far away from Duane.

God had me thinking in the right direction. Duane called at 6:00 a.m. Wednesday, October 7th, saying, "Mother, how soon can you get here?

I had a 4½ hour drive and I left in 3 hours, so I got there by 1:30 p.m. I did not return to Dallas until the 28th. Those were three weeks from Hell in many respects, and yet they were three of the best weeks of my life. Duane and I had some fabulous experiences as well as some terribly difficult times. He was the sweetest, most wonderful person to the very end. He never got hateful. He was accepting of each situation as it happened.

Things began to happen very quickly. He had an appointment that same afternoon at 2:30 p.m. with his Ophthalmologist. I did get there in time to take him. He was not feeling well, so we got him home as soon as we could.

Janice, Duane's home health nurse, came the next day about 10:00 a.m. His blood pressure was 104 over 90. He had a low grade fever and his heart rate was up to 120 from his normal 90. When I told her his appointment for his CT scan on his sinus was at 11:00 a.m., she was alarmed. She said, "We don't want him to have a heart attack."

She then called his primary doctor, who said he still needed to come in for a CAT scan of his head. The doctor asked to speak to me.

"Elaine, if I am correct," she said, "What is happening is worse than a heart attack." Man, that will make you step back a bit! At this point, I didn't ask any questions. We went to the clinic. He was miserably ill. They made us wait longer than I thought they should.

I went to the desk and said, "He has to have a place he can lie down. He is very ill." They took him in, did the scan, and we went home. That night I made a note, "Today was a sad day."

On Friday, the 9th, his doctor called to say the fungus had spread and had eaten into the cavity of the brain. She explained that he would probably go into a coma and then die. She thought she could control the pain. We were going to hit it with everything they knew to do, by using his central line to administer various medications. I did not tell Duane all of this.

On Sunday, we had another development. Duane said, "Mother, I can't see all your face." I think he could only see the center. I said, "Son, don't worry. We will get up in the morning and go see your eye doctor. We won't call for an appointment. I will make sure he sees you."

On Monday, the 12th, we went to the doctor's office the first thing. I was in combat mode, but I was nice. I am thankful that I was, because they were wonderful to us.

We saw a different doctor that morning. I was sitting so I was facing Duane in the examining chair. The doctor was very thorough; not saying a word. Then he went to the wash basin behind and to the side of where Duane was facing. I could see him completely. He had a very solemn face as he washed, and washed, and washed his hands. I knew instinctively that it was bad! I was right.

The doctor said, "Duane, I dilated your eyes, so I want you to wait in this room over here and I will be back in a few minutes to get you." I don't think Duane said anything. Bless his heart, in these last almost six years, he had heard so much bad news.

The doctor turned to me and said, "The fungus is pushing against the optical nerve. He is probably going to go blind in both eyes. We need to put him in the hospital and treat this very aggressively."

I appreciated what he was trying to do, but I said, "I need to call his primary doctor." I used his phone to call her. She agreed with me. She knew Duane did not want to go into the hospital. She didn't want to do that to him. She told me this was definitely going to take his life, but we would hit it with everything we knew to do.

"If you can administer the drugs and take care of him, let's let him stay home," she suggested. I told her that if the nurse could show me what to do, I could do it. Remember, I had no professional training for this, but every mother is a nurse, whether she knows it or not. Do you remember the story I told about my Daddy shaking my aunt and saying, "By God, you will stand it."? Well, before I went to Duane, I went into the ladies room and stood looking into the mirror, and wrapped my arms around myself and said, "By God's grace, you will stand this!"

I got Duane into the car, and then he asked. We had agreed long ago to be honest with each other. I told him the fungus had gone into his head, and that it was going to take his life. That was a lot to absorb.

There had been scary times before, but this was different. This was difficult for him to grasp. As we drove along, he said, "Well, Mother, I hope you don't care if I don't give up." I assured him I didn't; that he had been very ill before, and that we never know what God might do.

Even though we both knew this day would come, I am sure we were both in a state of shock. Now that I look back on it, I suppose I went into a survival mode, a Super Mother role. I had told him I would walk up to the door of death with him. Now I was not only going to have to do that, but I was going to be conducting advanced nursing responsibilities.

On the way home we stopped at the grocery store. Because of his vomiting and diarrhea, he had stayed away from sweets and soft drinks for a long time. He was on the scooter as we went through the store. I told him he could buy anything he wanted. Halloween was coming up, so he got decorated cup cakes and yes, soft drinks. I think he ended up eating only one of them, but the idea was that he could have it if he wanted it.

When we got home, we must have talked, but I don't remember that. I did call Dudley to let him know that if he wanted to see Duane before he went blind, he needed to come. He and Stephanie came down. Duane's father, Jim and Liz came also.

I called his caregivers from the church, his therapist, Shahn, and many other friends. They all came. Janice, his nurse came immediately and we began a plan for medication.

The next day, on the 13th, Duane went to the bathroom. We were going to give him a steroid. He got back into the bed, looking at me and at flowers which had been sent. He said, "I've been having sweet dreams." To which I replied, "Good." He continued, "This is all so lovely–so much trouble for me."

I asked, "Everyone coming to see you?"

"Yes."

"You are so easy to love. You are so special. Juan said you have an angel inside of you. Lester said, when God made Duane, He said, I'm going to put a little extra in him."

For only the second time, I gave him the steroid. I forgot to stop the pain medication. I started to get upset.

Duane said, "No problem, Mother. It's not fatal."

I made myself calm down, so I wouldn't upset him. Remember, I am not a nurse. We were dealing with a rather complicated routine. Sometimes I had to flush the line with saline and sometimes heparin before injecting meds into his line. Actually, looking back, I can't believe I did what I did. It truly was just the grace of God.

When I got in bed beside him, we touched hands. He was so relaxed. He seemed to dose a bit. In a few minutes he started clapping his hands quietly, and looking up he said, "Outstanding! Marvelous! Thank you!" I quietly responded, "You're welcome."

Later, he was smiling. I asked, "Sweet thoughts?" With more smiles, he said, "Yes." I almost felt as though I was intruding on some very special, private moments. Perhaps God was previewing Heaven for him. I think they were planning a fabulous welcoming party for him.

It was amazing that so many people came and yet they came at different times, so they all got to have some private time with Duane.

Oh, I almost forgot to tell you something very important. Duane got to thinking I had misunderstood what the doctors said. His sweet Nurse PA, Debra, came to the apartment to visit with him. As she went into his room I heard him say, "I think Mother over-reacted." Precious Debra had to tell him that I had not. This was actually going to take his life.

For over a year, I had been giving the testimony of my life at the church. I had told how God had always been there for me. I said, "There have been so many times that we thought Duane was going to die and he didn't. When he goes, I will know it is God's perfect time for him, and so I can accept it, although I know it will hurt tremendously."

Now, the rubber was hitting the road. Was I going to trust God to take Duane through the Valley of Death and come out on the other side in the presence of Jesus Christ? I could go through the shadow of the Valley, but right before Duane passed on, I would have to turn, and remain here on earth.

I do believe that if God had not given me my new family before taking Duane, I could have laid down beside him and closed my eyes in death with him. I believe I could have willed myself to die.

That was not the case though. I had too much to live for. I had a whole new family to love. I had my wonderful husband, Dudley, who stood by my side all the way, as well as our other children.

Yes, there were many special moments. I can still see the living room. Stephanie was sitting on the couch with Duane next to her. I believe Jim and Liz were there too. I was across the room. I tried to give Duane space to be with others when they were there. He and I had lots of alone times those next two weeks. Duane leaned over and put his head in Stephanie's lap. It truly was a beautiful sister and brother moment!

It was a long, rigorous 13 days. There was lots of laughter between Duane and me. I already told you how we laughed over my resigning as his Mother.

We talked a lot about Heaven and the people he would see there. I explained to him that the Bible tells us that God sends angels to accompany us into the presence of Jesus. Can you see why I say it is so important to have someone with us at our death, whom we can trust?

If I had ever backed away from what the Bible says about anything, he wouldn't be able to trust me either. I still thank God every day that He kept me strong. I also thank God that He has forgiven me of all my sins. I am like Paul. I sometimes feel I am the chief of sinners.

Juan was so faithful to come. On Friday Duane had two seizures. Once, I was on one side of the bed. He had tea in his hand, and suddenly, he began to shake; tea went everywhere. At first I thought he was dying. When the seizure ended, I was on the other side of the bed, holding him. I have no idea how I got there. It was a terrible experience. It was caused by medication. We made adjustments and that never happened again. Juan came and spent the night. That helped me.

One day Duane was seeing things that weren't real, but I helped him realize they were not real. He saw little fairies on my back. We laughed about that. I told him that I would protect him. God always seemed to give me the right thing to say to him to calm him.

Dudley had two weddings on Saturday the 17th, so I don't think he came back to Houston until the following week. He phoned every day. He was wonderful support through not only those last two weeks, but for two years. I can't imagine how we would have gotten along without him.

Saturday was a very busy day. I happened to note some of Duane's visitors that day. His housekeeper, Beverly came. She may have cleaned that day. Barbara and Olga came from his church. I think it was Barbara who said she didn't know how I was doing what I was doing. I said, "Well, I would like to tell you I am just a marvelous person, but the truth is, it is Jesus in me." I think it was she who said to me as she was leaving, "Duane leaves such a legacy of love."

Later that night when I told him what Barbara said, Duane replied, "Well, isn't that what we are here for?" I thought that said a lot about who he was. He had always been a loving person, but in those last two years, God really perfected him in love.

I think Shahn came that day too. In fact, she and Libby both came several times those two weeks. Truly, he was loved by so many. Libby stayed Saturday night. I slept from 2:00 a.m. until

The Final Days

8:00 a.m. I got up several times, but went right back to the couch. If you ever want to help a family, that is a great service. Sit with their loved one, so they can get a little rest.

Libby did laundry that day too. He had soiled his bed three or four times. Libby made a run to the store and got some Depends for my little darling.

When he awoke and saw them, he asked, "When did this happen?" I said, "Honey, you were in such a deep sleep, you didn't realize you needed to go, so we put those plastic briefs on you for comfort." He was so good! He just accepted whatever I said.

Once we were trying to get the sheet out from under him, so we could clean him up. Bless his heart, he looked up at me and said, "Tell me what the goal is and maybe I can help." We told him and believe it or not, we all chuckled, and he did help. There never was a better patient. By the way, I think it is demeaning to refer to Depends as diapers.

As I said earlier, from time to time, he would say, "Well, this is my reality for now." I have found that phrase very helpful in my own life. I pray it will help you.

Libby asked Duane something that night. He replied, "I don't know. Ask Mother, she is in charge." Just think, after some really rocky years, we ended in such a beautiful place.

Duane's friend, Larry, came on Sunday. Duane was not doing very well by then. Larry told me a cute story. He said, "I thought he was out of it," but he said, "Come here, let me show you something." Duane dragged himself out of bed to show off the new clothes we had bought for him. Most of them still had the price tags on them when he died, but it was worth the money we spent to see how happy he was the night we had our dinner party, just three weeks prior.

Duane was in and out of reality all day. Once he said, "That should have helped you." He continued, "Let's pray for those men working on the skyscraper." (He was in his own world.) Nevertheless, I prayed. Then I asked, "Would you like me to say a prayer for you?" Quickly he replied, "Sure." So I did; of course, I did.

Later that day, I asked if he wanted me to dial Juan. He smiled, then laughed. I ask "What?" He said, "I can dial." I bent down, hugged him, and told him what a great person he was. That was maybe 30–45 seconds. By then, he had forgotten he was going to call and lay the phone down.

That Sunday, his father called. I said, "I'm here! I'm hanging in." Shortly after that, Duane was almost out of bed. He said he was looking for papers to return his compact stereo. There was no plan to return it; his mind was just going constantly. We were keeping him in bed because he had not eaten anything since Tuesday night. He did still have his TPN, but his body was getting weaker.

By this time, David at Option Care, and I were becoming friends. They were providing all Duane's drugs, which were highly controlled. I would call and tell them what we needed. It seems like they came every day or two.

As we got closer to Duane's death, David told me about some of the physical things which might happen. It helped so much to be aware of the possibilities, some of which happened.

Despite the stress of very little sleep, lots of high-tech nursing responsibilities, and the emotional toll this was taking on both me and Duane, we still had some very tender and even funny moments that last week.

He was propped up in bed much of the time. I would sit there, shoulder to shoulder. Sometimes I would hold him, but often that last week, he would hold me.

Once he said, "We will talk more, but there is nothing left to be said. We have taken care of everything." Often we comforted each other just by holding each other, or holding hands. We were both such touching people, that just our touching was comforting to us.

One time while sitting in bed, he began to laugh out loud. When I asked what was so funny, he said, "Look, look at my teeny, little arms." He had learned to see humor in life. I was so proud of him!

Another day, we were sitting there and he asked, "Who is that in the bathroom with Beverly?" I said, "Honey, no one is here but us, and Beverly, who is here to clean." He insisted, "Mother, I see a man in there."

All at once it hit me. I said, "Duane I am sure you do see someone. I am sure he is an angel. I told you that God would send angels to escort you into the presence of Jesus. We have talked about the fact you are transitioning from this world to the next. That is why the angel is visible to you and not to me. It's God's way of assuring you that He is going to take care of you, and that there is nothing to fear."

I mentioned how absolutely wonderful David, with Option Care was to me. One night, maybe around 2:00 a.m., Duane's pain pump stopped working. I was panic stricken. I not only didn't know what to do, but if you knew how inept I am with mechanical things, you would understand my fear. As Duane had said, "I was in charge," so I had to "fix" it.

I called David. He calmed me, and very patiently walked me through the process and together, we got it working again. This was not easy. It took me several tries.

During the last week I called the funeral home and put them on alert. His doctor didn't think this would go on for very long. We got a number of phone calls from friends. One of Dud's long-time friends, Sam Choate, called from Florida to check on us. Jim's brother, Duane's Uncle Bill called. The calls, the prayers, the visitors all did help. If nothing else, they were distractions for a few minutes.

Another nice distraction was a large picture puzzle which was on Duane's dining table. It was nice to just stop by every now and then and look for a piece to put into the picture. Duane and I both enjoyed putting them together. Somehow, this reminds me of life. If Dudley were here, he would say, "Now that'll preach!" For those of you who don't know, that is Southern for that will.

Toward the end of the second week, Duane was beginning to have some pressure pain in his head. We were controlling the acute pain, but the pressure was harder to control.

Dud came back to Houston sometime that week; Mike came too. On Thursday or Friday, Duane received a package containing some comic books he had ordered. He had quite a collection. He realized that he couldn't see well enough to read them. Someone went out and bought a magnifying sheet. We all hoped it would work, but it didn't.

Wonderful Dudley sat on the bed with him and read comics to him. He loved doing it and it made Duane very happy. This gave Dud another chance to be a "real dad" to our little boy. He was reading to him as though he were just a child. Dud's love was so healing to Duane. It completed something inside of me, too.

I had tried so hard to find him a good daddy, and I had made many mistakes. God had something in mind all along. If only I could have known in that labor room so long ago when I cried out, "Oh, Dudley, hold my hand," that he would be that baby's daddy at the end of his life.

As I have often said, "God only tells me on an "as needs to know" basis and most of the time, He doesn't think I need to know.

On Friday, the 23rd, Shahn, Duane's therapist and friend, came to see him. She was going out of town and wanted to say goodbye in case he left us before she got back. They had a sweet visit. He was more concerned about her, than himself.

Sometime that week, I had been injecting something into his line, when he looked up at me, and smiling, said, "Mother, don't think I am so self-absorbed, that I don't know what this is doing to you." I bent down and told him how much I loved him, and once again, we both vowed to love each other through all eternity!

I pray that if you have someone special in your life; be it a child, a parent, a sibling, or anyone, if that person knows Jesus Christ as their Savior, no matter how "off the track" they get, Jesus will bring them back into the fold. For those of you who do not know Jesus, I pray that you will do your own investigation and see for yourself if He won't prove to be trustworthy.

To be honest, I don't know how people bury their loved ones, if they don't know that they will one day be together again in the presence of God the Father, Jesus the Son, and the Holy Spirit. I can see why people who do not believe turn to alcohol or drugs, or become bitter, dried-up people. My heart goes out to them.

Friday night Juan came over to see how we were doing. This was taking a great toll on him, too. He did truly love Duane and had been good to him.

Sometime during those last weeks, Duane did tell me that he should have married this one specific girl. He said, "She would have made a good wife and mother." He went on to say they could have been happy together.

Juan had a busy week and he was really tired. He lay down on top of the covers by Duane and drifted off to sleep. Here might be a good place to say thank you to all the gay people I have known personally. They have never been demonstrative with their affections in front of me. I appreciate that very much.

After Juan had drifted off Duane said, very excitedly, "Mother, we have some Citovene in the refrigerator." I sat down beside him and said, "Son, I am sorry. Citoveen won't fix what's wrong with your eyes. We have tried everything, but nothing has stopped the fungus. Honey, you have always said that if you went blind, you didn't want to live. Last week they told me I could stop your TPN and you would probably go in a few days. I know you must feel out of control, but you are still in control. I won't make those decisions as long as you can make them. You have been so brave and fought so hard to stay alive, and been such a wonderful person through it all. If the pressure in your head gets to be too much or you are too tired to fight anymore, you can stop the TPN. It would not be committing suicide; it would be letting nature take care of itself. It is all your decision and I am here for you all the way."

After thinking for a minute or two, he said, "I think I will see how the weekend goes. Then on Monday, I will call Debra and see what direction I am going in and how fast. I know she will tell me the truth and then I will make a decision." God was gracious to us. He made the decision for us.

I don't really remember much about Saturday. I do think that was the night I woke up and realized Duane was out of bed. I said, "Oh, Honey, let me help you. He was in the kitchen. He said, "I'm hungry." I guess he was. He hadn't eaten for days. I don't remember what he got, but some little something, and then back to bed he went.

The other thing I remember was calling my sister, Pat. She is a great prayer warrior and I was so tired and I needed someone to pray for strength for me to see this through to the end. We talked awhile, and then she prayed. Pat and I don't talk that often, but we always know we can call the other for prayer. Looking back over my life, I see that God puts different people in our lives for different reasons. We are all here to serve each other. As Duane said, "Isn't that what we are here for?"

CHAPTER 13

Our Last Day—then Heaven

* * *

By Sunday morning, October 25, 1998, both Duane and I were totally exhausted, physically and mentally. We had maybe never been stronger spiritually. He was ready to go, as you will hear in his own words. I was ready to let him go, because I hated seeing him suffer.

Some might ask, "Are you really ready to let go?" The honest answer is both "yes" and "no". I will tell you it is easier when you know their destination.

A few days earlier, I had said, "Son, you do understand, don't you, that the very instant you leave my presence, you will be in the presence of Jesus?" His reply was simple, "I have heard that." I responded, "You can believe it. That is what the Bible tells us. For believers in Jesus as our Savior, it states, 'to be absent from the body, is to be present with the Lord.' You don't have to wonder for one second." That is what it comes down to at the end of life.

You notice that my style of writing is done in very simple language. I have not tried to impress you with lofty words or complicated sentence structure. Our story is simple. It is a story of unconditional love, even with boundaries, and of total trust because I stood on what I believed to be true. My experience with death tells me that it is super important that we have someone we can trust when we are looking death straight in the face. Duane trusted me so completely, that when I assured him of my love, God's love, and his destination to Jesus, he could relax and receive death, not fight it.

Now, that is the "yes" part of letting them go. This is the "no" answer.

We know we are going to miss them every day for the rest of our lives. I once heard it said, "You never have closure. That isn't possible. You just have to go on and you learn to live with it."

This is another way to put it. On one of my last business trips, I had finished my meetings and had collapsed in a chair. I was just sort of staring out into space. All at once I thought, "I am going to miss being known."

That's right, Duane knew me better than anyone other than God. He knew my strengths, my weaknesses, my attributes, and my flaws. He knew my faith beliefs, my political beliefs, and my work ethics. He embraced most of how I saw life and understood that any differences we had never affected or diminished my love for him.

Yes, this kind of support is very hard to give up. I lost my wonderful husband, Dudley, through death in 2006. He was like Duane; he knew all my faults and had watched all my mistakes and failures and still thought I was absolutely amazing. He wrote me poetry that made me want to be a better person.

That's what Duane and Dudley did for me. They made me want to be better than I am. Of course, this is what my Lord has always done for me. I never wanted to disappoint Him or my mother as I was growing up.

As I said, on our last day together I was totally exhausted, deep to the bone. You may remember, I had been there since the 7th and this was the 25th. We had been through a lot. Duane was asleep, so I thought I would grab a quick nap. We were alone, so everything was quiet. I fell into a deep sleep and slept for an hour or so.

When I awoke, I was horrified! He had used the bedpan and left it on the corner of the bed. I couldn't believe he had to do that for himself, without me to help him.

I had wanted to do this job all by myself out of love, but who knows, is there a little false pride there too? Truly, I don't know.

All my life, from the time I was eight years old, I was told to be brave. That attitude has served me well and also has served a lot of other people well through me.

At any rate, I suddenly knew I was going to have to ask for help. Physically, I was almost at the end of my rope. Around 10:00 or 10:30 a.m., one of Duane's friends, Libby, came by to check on us. I knew she could use some money, so I asked her if I could hire her to stay with Duane every other night. I told her that since I could trust her completely, I could sleep deeply. I knew she would awaken me if she needed me. She agreed to come back that night around 9:00 or 10:00 p.m...I felt better, knowing I had a plan.

Libby must have left about noon, because Duane and I were alone the last four or five hours of his life. His doctor thought he might go this weekend. She thought he would probably go into a coma before he left us. I was blessed, as he was with me right up until the time he left. This is how it happened.

I was not only wide awake now, but it was as though my senses were heightened to a new intense level. It seemed Duane and I were both in a new spiritual arena. I had told him that I would walk up to the door of death with him. This was exactly what I was doing. Don't feel sorry for me that I was alone with him. That is how I wanted it; although I hadn't really thought it all through. I just knew I didn't want either of us distracted by anyone else.

A day or two before when I realized how badly things were going, I went into his office next to his bedroom. I looked up, closed my eyes, and pleadingly ask for God's help.

It was a simple prayer, "God, help me, help You, get him from here to there." This was my goal; to get Duane safely into the arms of our Lord.

That afternoon Duane was sitting up and I was standing beside him. He looked up at me and said, "I can't believe I've done this to myself." I just bent down, hugged him to myself, and said, "I love you son!"

The next day as I was telling Dudley about our afternoon, I said, "That was a confession. Some people walk down the aisle and say, "I am a sinner and need a Savior." The thief on the cross said, "Remember me when You come into Your kingdom."

Duane said, "I can't believe I've done this to myself." He took responsibility for his behavior. He left this world with a sweet attitude. He did not blame God, or the person who gave him AIDS, or his dad for leaving, or me for not being a perfect mother. That was one of the proudest moments of my life. What a fine young man he had grown into. Look around today. Hardly anyone wants to take responsibility for their actions.

Later as Duane was sitting up and looking up, almost past the ceiling, he said, "Let's get this thing going! Let's get off the ground!" Immediately, I thought of the song, *I'll Fly Away*. He was not irrational or hallucinating, so I felt he was definitely leaving me soon.

He leaned back onto his pillow saying he would try to rest. His breathing had become labored. I had administered pain medication as instructed. In fact, I was not giving it quite as often as I could have.

Earlier in the week someone said to me, "Just get in there as often as you can and give him a shot." I did not want to think I had anything to do with his time of death. That was God's deal. While he was uncomfortable, he did not seem to be in pain.

In a few minutes, I said, "I will rub your feet. That usually helps you relax." As I rubbed, he said, "Mother, sing to me." So I sang *Jesus Loves Me* and a couple of the old hymns. Then with a smile in his voice, he said so sweetly, "Mother, can we have that upbeat music from yesterday?"

I loved it. I chuckle as I think of it. Even as he lies there dying, he still asks with a sense of humor for more "fun" music. It was the praise tape sent to me from the Renewing the Heart Conference by Focus on the Family.

I put the music on for him. Duane was too weak to move as much as yesterday, but he did wiggle his toes some and his fingers occasionally. After a few minutes, I left my post at his feet and stood by his side. I could see we were getting closer to the end. Don't ask me how I knew, I just did.

As his labored breathing moved his chest up and down, in and out, his bones pressed against his thin little chest wall. I could see every bone as though I were looking at an X-ray. Then the most amazing thought came to my mind! God was allowing my beloved son to die in the same way His Son died! During crucifixion, they have to push up with their legs in order to breathe. In the end, I have been told they suffocate. God was honoring my son and blessing me by the way he died. I am sure this does not mean anything to some of you. That is okay. It simply means God was being good to both of us.

Once he looked up at me from his pillow and said, "God loves me, doesn't He?" I said, "Yes, He does." Very seriously he said, "He has always loved me, hasn't He?" Again, I replied with great feeling, "Yes, son, always." He then asked, "Even when I was being bad?" Quickly, I responded, "Oh yes, Honey, even when we are bad, because that is when we need it most." He seemed satisfied. Remember, he had re-confessed his belief in Jesus Christ in January.

I was not surprised when a little later, Duane said, "Mother, I am so hot." I replied, "Honey, it helps you when we put a cool cloth on your chest. I will get one for you."

Then he said some of the sweetest words I ever heard, "Come here first Mother." He rose up a little as I bent down. We gave each other a huge, big, wonderful bear hug. We rubbed each other's back and once again we vowed to love each other through all eternity!

Then I went for the cloth, not realizing I had just said goodbye to my precious baby boy, my beloved son in whom I am well pleased. (I borrowed that last phrase from our Heavenly Father. That is what He said about Jesus Christ at Jesus' baptism.) I am pretty sure God doesn't mind. I think He loves it when we copy Him.

I returned, putting the cloth on Duane's chest, and standing ever so quietly. All at once the music stopped playing. I thought, "Oh, no, the music has stopped!"

I couldn't move though. It was as though my feet were riveted to the floor. His face flushed and his tiny, thin, little body shuddered as it shut down. I thought, "Oh, God, is he going to have a seizure again?" Soon, I realized, it was over. He was gone, but, no, not lost. I knew then and know now where he is. He is with our Lord.

Since I had seen a couple of people die before this, I came to understand death differently. I used to think that we died and then our soul went to be with Jesus. Now, I know that our soul leaves our body, and then it shuts down since it is no longer needed. I am sure that Duane left while I was getting the wash cloth. He knew he was leaving and that is why he asked for a hug and wanted to give me a hug to remember forever and ever.

Stop, and think with me. For a Christian Mom, it doesn't get any better than for her son to meet Jesus while listening to a "praise to Jesus" tape. How great is that! Not great that he left me, but great that he left in this manner.

All this took place over a couple of hours. In many respects, it seemed longer. It was painful and at the same time it was satisfying to be able to assure Duane that not only did I love him unconditionally, but so did God and that He always had loved him. That was really the most important part. It was also very comforting to both of us to re-state that we would love each other through all eternity. We both knew we were parting, but only for a time.

I was still alone with Duane, but there was work to be done. Just now, as I wrote this, I sobbed and sobbed. Back then, I did what had to be done. First, I went to the hall and wrote on his chart, which I had maintained those last weeks, "4:00 p.m. - Xpired." My writing was a little shaky, but not much.

Next, I called the Physician's Assistant. Those were the instructions I had. I could not reach her, but left a message. Next I called Dudley. He and Stephanie came that night. Then, of course, I called Jim and Liz. After I made those first calls, I made Duane look comfortable by straightening his head and taking care of his lines.

What I did next will seem very strange to some of you, but some of you will "really get it." I went back to his office, looked up with my eyes wide open and raising my arms in a sign of praise and victory I said, "We did it! We did it! We got Duane from here with me to there with You! Thank You, Father! Thank You for saving my baby!"

For all who read this book, let me share with you what I said for the first time at the memorial service we had for Duane in Houston. I knew most of those people did not share my faith. They knew what I believed, but I never really tried to change them. They watched me live out my faith. That day I said to them and I say to all of you, "Your faith may be different from mine. You may express it differently than I do. I pray your faith gives you the comfort mine gives me."

After thanking God, I called my friend David. I knew he would want to know and also knew he would say words of comfort. To my surprise, Duane's nurse, Janice, was also there. She was appalled that I was alone and came right over.

Since I had not heard from the doctor or assistant, I was forced to call 911. The doctor had not wanted me to go through all this, but so be it. We all do what we have to do, right?

The precious firemen came through the doors with paddles in the air. I stepped in front of the hall and said, "He is a do not resuscitate. Here are the papers." Remember, this was 1998. The papers were signed in 1993. The fireman said, "These are very old."

For a minute, in my state of grief, I thought he was questioning their validity. I nearly gasped as I said, "Yes." Then he quickly said, "He has been sick a long time." I agreed and he waved off the other firemen with their paddles. Next, he asked what time he had died and I showed him my very complete chart.

By this time, it was almost 6:00 p.m., so Duane had been gone two hours. To be official, he did, of course, make a professional exam. The death certificate shows the time of death at 4:00 p.m. I am thankful that I kept such detailed records.

Since Duane died at home, the police came, and they called the medical examiner. They had to wait for the medical examiner to call back. I will tell you, if you die on Sunday afternoon, it is likely no one will be available. That is, no one but God.

Okay, I think it is time for you to catch a breath. I know this is heavy, but it is our story, and it is so meaningful. Really, God's timing was so kind to us. We were alone. He and I worked so hard to carry Duane for nine months and here we were, the three of us, alone again, working to see Duane off to be with Jesus. Also, do you remember that Duane was going to call Debra, the PA, on Monday to determine if we should disconnect the feeding supply? We didn't have to make that kind of a hard decision.

Picture this scene if you can. My baby is gone, but his body is still in the other room. I am wiped out. Janice has gone, but Duane's friend, Libby has returned. The fireman and policeman will not have a seat. They are standing at attention like they are on guard at a castle; stiff as boards, sober, very nice, but in total silence. This, of course, reflects their training.

Back home, our pastor, Stan, has been having us recite a little affirmation. So, I say, "Okay guys. We are going to play a game. I am going to say, 'God is good.' and you are going to reply, 'All the time.' Then I am going to say, 'All the time' and you will reply, 'God is good'."

I know you can hardly believe what you are reading and I am sure they couldn't believe their ears. Here is the really amazing part! They actually went along with me! We repeated that saying several times. They were probably afraid that if they didn't, I would fall apart on them and have some screaming nervous breakdown.

Perhaps, what they didn't realize was that the words we were saying reflected exactly what I was feeling. God is good all the time, no matter what. To say that aloud in times of trouble has a soothing, very calming affect on us. Try it sometime. It really does work!

I am sure that story has been repeated many times in the stations of both the fireman and policeman. They no doubt say, "This woman's son had died and she had been alone with him. By the time we got there, she had flipped out!" Oh, well, it gives them something to talk about on long boring nights.

Finally, we are told the body could be released to the funeral home. I had already made the arrangements and had them on alert. They came about 8:00 p.m. Libby was still there. There were two men in dark suits, looking very stiff and uncomfortable and unhappy that they had to pull this duty.

After a few minutes of discomfort, I said, "I am sure that you would rather be any place but here on a Sunday night. I am sorry you had to come out and I thank you for coming."

Later, Libby said, "I watched in awe at how you melted those men."

We all have our limits. After all I had done so bravely, I said to Libby, "I can't watch them take my baby." She walked me out into the parking lot and stood so that she could see when they were gone. I can't remember, but I am sure she stayed until Dudley and Stephanie got there, which was probably about 10:00 that night.

I don't want to make Duane's story sound like it is all about me. Yes, he and I were the main characters, but there were hundreds of people whose lives he touched and for the most part, in a very positive way. Stephanie and Mike had grown up with Duane. Stephanie and Duane had some close times not only when they were young, but also in college.

Even though Duane had not experienced a close relationship with his father, Jim, this was still a loss for Jim. In fact, in his mind he maybe thought they were close. There is a saying, "perception is reality." Jim's perception of their relationship may have been different from Duane's. They just never spent much time together. They never shared the same interests.

Duane's death was a great loss to Dudley. He was sorry that he had not tried harder to guide Duane away from the homosexual lifestyle when he was young.

However, the greatest thing Dudley did for Duane was to be a real daddy to him those last two years of his life. It was just natural for him to love Duane. He didn't have to work at it.

Duane often said, "When Dad (meaning Dudley) calls me Son, I just melt."

They truly meant the world to each other. Dudley knew how to father a son, because he and Mike were so very close. It was easy for them to draw Duane into their inner circle; which leads me to speak of Mike. Because of Mike's special relationship with his father, he could have been jealous of Dudley's love for Duane. I don't believe he ever felt that way. He knew there was room in Dudley's heart for both of them. How sad it is when people do not understand that "hearts are made of stretchy material." That quote came from a friend of mine, Billie Aylor.

I can't speak of losses without mentioning the man who Duane was in a relationship with at the end of his life. Juan was very devoted to Duane. He had given up a promotion to stay in Houston to be near Duane.

After all these years, Juan and I still stay in touch. He calls me on all the holidays, on my birthday, on Duane's birthday and date of his death, and even Mother's Day. I still think of him as another son.

Someone once said to me, "The worst thing you ever did was to take him to that Baptist Church." He was referring to First Baptist Dallas. He was wrong. For you see, Duane heard the truth there and developed his relationship with Jesus there.

Yes, he walked away, but after making his mistakes, and living out the consequences of them, he had a place to come home to… the love of God, the arms of his mother, and Jesus, The Christ.

Now Duane is basking in the warmth and glow of Jesus' love and will be there throughout all eternity, totally loved, and totally forgiven.

My Last Letter to Duane:

Dear Duane,

I hope that you and God are pleased with what I have written, your story, our story, God's story. I can still see you and hear your words, "Mother, I want you to go educate the world." You knew what I would say and that I would be as truthful as I could be, even about all my blemishes as a human being. God demanded I write it. I pray that He approves. Tell everyone there in Heaven that I said, "Hi! And that I love them all. Sing an extra praise song to Jesus from me. Truly, you are my beloved son! I am so grateful God chose me for your mother. I'll see you soon, Honey.

Your loving Mother, (through all eternity)

Yes, one day I will join him, and what a glorious day that will be! Won't you come and join us?

APPENDIX
Assurance of Heaven

* * *

For those of you who would like to know how you can be assured of going to heaven, you might read the following verses in the Bible.

- John 3:16 says, "For God so loved the world, that He gave his one and only Son, that whoever believes in Him shall not perish, but have eternal life."
- Romans 3:23 talks about how we all are sinners. "For all have sinned, and fall short of the glory of God."
- Romans 6:23 states that the penalty for sin is death: "For the wages of sin is death but the gift of God is eternal life in Jesus Christ our Lord."
- Romans 5:8 explains that we may come to Christ just as we are: "But God demonstrates His love toward us in that while we were yet sinners, Christ died for us."
- Romans 10:9, 10, & 13 explain that we can confess, believe, pray and receive God's gift of Jesus Christ and his sacrifice for us: "That if you confess with your mouth, 'Jesus is Lord' and believe in your heart that God raised him from the dead, you will be saved. For it is with your heart that you believe and are justified and it is with your mouth that you confess and are saved."

If you wish to receive God's free gift of eternal life, just tell Him that you accept what Christ did for you and ask Him to guide you with your life.

I encourage you to find a church which teaches that Jesus Christ is the Savior of the world, including you.

Made in the USA
San Bernardino, CA
26 February 2014